STEVEN. SHARON
& ELLIE -
5/2/12.

DENIS LAW

MY LIFE IN FOOTBALL

DENIS LAW

MY LIFE IN FOOTBALL

with Ivan Ponting

SIMON &
SCHUSTER

London · New York · Sydney · Toronto · New Delhi

A CBS COMPANY

First published in Great Britain by Simon & Schuster UK Ltd, 2011
A CBS COMPANY

3 5 7 9 10 8 6 4 2

Simon & Schuster UK Ltd
1st Floor
222 Gray's Inn Road
London
WC1X 8HB

www.simonandschuster.co.uk

Simon & Schuster Australia, Sydney
Simon & Schuster India, New Delhi

A CIP catalogue record for this book is available
from the British Library

Hardback ISBN 978-0-85720-084-6
Scottish Edition Hardback ISBN 978-0-85720-146-1

Text design and layout by Imran Haq
Typeset by M Rules
Printed and bound in Italy by
LEGO S.pA

CONTENTS

FOREWORD
BY SIR ALEX FERGUSON

I've heard Denis Law described as the greatest Scottish footballer since the war, and unquestionably he is just that. But, for me, even such a mighty accolade doesn't do the man justice.

Obviously – at least I hope it's obvious! – I'm not old enough to have watched and assessed such timeless heroes of the far-distant past as Alex James, Hugh Gallacher, Alex Jackson or Alan Morton, the 'Wee Blue Devil' who tormented England so famously at Wembley in 1928. Clearly these were magnificent performers whose names will live forever in the annals of the game, but I find it impossible to imagine that any of them could have topped the Aberdeen fisherman's son to whom not one, but *two* statues have been raised at Old Trafford. So as far as I'm concerned, Denis Law is the best Scottish player of all time, bar nobody.

At this point I have to admit that, although I'm only a couple of years younger than Denis, he has always been my hero. For me, as I grew up in Glasgow as a young centre-forward making my way with Queen's Park, he epitomised everything a striker should be.

He had astonishing physical courage, unbelievably sharp reactions and all the talent in the world. He was so exciting and he projected a certain panache, a crackling cocktail of aggression and style in the very way he moved, the way he held himself. You had only to glance at him to know he was a Scotsman – he could start a scrap in an empty house, he would fight his own shadow. He was only a slim boy, but he would square up to the most fearsome centre-halves, giants with bulging muscles who made me think of Bluto, the hulking villain from the Popeye cartoon show, and he never so much as flinched.

He thrilled crowds everywhere he went, scything through defences like a claymore through porridge, spinning on a sixpence and tucking away chances that he had no right to even reach. Then there was his incredible spring, and a seeming ability to hang in the air as if in suspended animation before dispatching his headers. Just look at his goal from a near-post corner against England at Hampden in 1966 (opposite) – he's towering above everyone from a standing start. That's what I call greatness.

I'm not ashamed to say that I used to try to copy him, not so much in the way I played, but by pulling down my sleeves and wiping my nose on them during the breaks in the action. It didn't turn me into Denis Law, but it made me feel good, and I knew I was imitating the best there was.

He started his professional career as a 16-year-old with Huddersfield Town, making a startling impact at a time when English football was enjoying some of its halcyon days. He was still only 20 when Manchester City bought him for a British record fee of £55,000. Equate that to the modern transfer market and you're talking about £30-odd million, the equivalent of Manchester United buying Wayne Rooney, which tells you all you need to know about the phenomenal progress he was making.

Denis won his first cap against Wales at the age of 18, which amazed people who had seen pictures of him as a pale, skinny little schoolboy wearing spectacles and with a turn in his eye. The first time I saw him was three weeks later in his second international, against Northern Ireland at Hampden, and I had no doubt I was in the presence of someone special. You had to be quite something to play for Scotland as a teenager in those days, and Denis was in the vanguard of what would become the national side's golden period, featuring the likes of Jim Baxter, Dave Mackay, John White, Alex Young, Ian St John and Billy Bremner. Aye, we had some fantastic footballers back then, and it almost makes me weep to compare that vintage with the Scotland teams of modern times.

Of course, in footballing terms, Denis was always an Anglo, and that cost him dear in terms of appearances. As far as the people who picked the side were concerned, every time Scotland lost a game it was Denis Law's fault. They always blamed the Anglos and that used to make me laugh because, in general, apart from Baxter before he joined Sunderland, all the best players were Anglos.

If ever a man deserved to parade his talents on the grandest stage it was Denis, but sadly Scotland lost the qualifier for the 1962 World Cup to Czechoslovakia, who went on to meet Brazil in the final, which hinted at what might have been achieved.

That didn't prevent him being recognised as one of the planet's top footballers, though, as he was selected alongside true greats such as Alfredo di Stefano, Ferenc

Puskas and Eusebio for the Rest of the World side which met England as part of the FA's centenary celebrations in 1963. It was no surprise that he stood out even in that rarefied company, scoring a terrific goal.

In time he went on to become one of the most beloved and fêted of all Manchester United footballers – and that's saying something – but maybe most precious to me are my personal memories of the man. For instance, there was the first time I met him, at a game in Paris. We were sat in a café at the Parc des Princes when in walked Sigi Held. I don't know why I did it, but something prompted me to ask him for his autograph and I was staggered when the German international refused me. My raw reaction was along the lines of 'F****** hell, who do you think you are, Denis Law?' Denis looked up and asked me if I was taking the p***, but I wasn't. I was just employing a saying we used in Scotland if somebody got carried away with themselves. It was something which indicated the colossal regard in which Denis was held.

Then there was the time when a Scottish football delegation was staying in the

Palace of Versailles and I got into an argument in my room with a fellow about apartheid in South Africa. It raged on and on, and Denis gently attempted to rescue me. But I just wouldn't give in, so he shrugged his shoulders, lay back on my bed and smoked his pipe as he watched me getting slaughtered. That image of Denis, relaxing contentedly with the smoke curling round his head, remains vivid in my memory to this day.

So does his typically impish grin when he greeted me at the Cliff on the morning after we had won our first Premier League title in 1993. I'd previously asked him why he never turned up to see our training and he'd said the last person I needed at the ground was Denis Law. I could understand his reasoning, thinking that the players mightn't want him there when United hadn't won the League for a quarter of a century. But he made me a promise – win the League and the next day I'll be there. Well, I didn't get to bed until six in the morning after we'd won, but when I took myself to work four hours later, there he was, sipping a cup of tea, looking as pleased as punch.

Denis is a lovely man and he was an absolutely fabulous footballer. Anyone who has the slightest doubt about his stature in the game might care to heed the words of no less eminent a judge than Pelé, who once said that the only British player who could possibly get into the Brazil team was Denis Law. I rest my case.

Sir Alex Ferguson,
September 2011

CHAPTER 1

A WEE
SPINDLY
LAD

LEFT: If I'm looking a wee bit gormless here as a 12-year-old, I can assure you the reality was far worse. This is long before the age of airbrushing photographs, but the old newspapermen had their own equivalent – a heavy black pencil. My eyes look impeccably straight in this shot, but in fact I had a terrible squint, and it appears the sports editor was keen to hide that from his readers. That was all right by me, because I hated being called Cock-Eye by the other kids, so much so that to play football I took my glasses off, closed my right eye and played with the view afforded by my left. Mind, if anyone threw that name at me then I'd kick them. You had to stand up for yourself, and the fact that I had the squint made me battle that little bit harder.

I'm sure this was taken just after I started secondary school, because I recognise my new grey windcheater. I was the last of a fisherman's seven children, so there was never any money to spare, and Mum paid for our clothes on tick, on the slate. A guy would call round every week to collect a shilling, or whatever, that she had somehow scraped together. It was a different world back then.

ABOVE: Lining up with the lads and lasses of the Kitty Brewster primary school in Aberdeen in 1950, when I was ten. I'm second from the left on the back row, trying desperately to disguise my squint with what might charitably be described as a quizzical grin. I recognise most of the faces, but I have to be honest and admit that I can remember only one name, that of David Lane, standing next to the teacher. Nearly all the boys are wearing ties, possibly because that was expected every day, more likely because our mothers knew the picture was being taken and made a special effort to smarten us up for the occasion.

ALEX DAWSON:

Despite the difference in our sizes, Denis was just three days younger than me, and at this age he wasn't always sure of his place in our team. But when I bumped into him again a few years later in a youth game between Manchester United and Huddersfield, he was a player and a half. He hadn't grown much, but he looked like ripping us apart every time he got the ball. Unfortunately we never lined up together at Old Trafford – I left a few months before he arrived.

ABOVE: Just look at the size of Alex Dawson, the lad with the ball at his feet in the front row of the Aberdeen Schoolboys team round about 1953. That's me next to him on his left, the little fella with the sparrow's legs. Alex went on to score a lot of goals for Manchester United, but he left Old Trafford during the season before I arrived, so we never had the chance to link up again. He went on to have a fine career in the Football League, notably at Preston, but maybe he didn't quite achieve all that was expected of him. He had been pitchforked into the United team when he was very young because of the Munich disaster, and that might have hindered his development in the long term.

At the time of this picture he was an exceptional performer. Such was his strength and stature, he was turning out for the Under-15s when he was only 13, something that nobody had done before. Off the pitch he was lovely, very gentle, but on it he was a fearsome opponent, a tough, bustling centre-forward, and I was always glad he was on my side. Soon after this Alex moved to England, because his father was a trawlerman who found work in Hull.

ABOVE: As you might gather from the look of fierce concentration on my face as I line up a shot at the goal guarded by my pal George Ingram, I used to take my Subbuteo rather seriously. Every Friday night I would go next door to the house of Sid Thompson, the leader of the Aberdeen Lads' Club, and invariably the competition was intense, to put it mildly. I always put everything I had into any game I took up. Whatever I was playing, then I wanted to win. It might be noticed that George is laughing here – but I'm not!

Of course, we had to keep all our fingers on the table, except for the one that was flicking the ball, otherwise it was a foul. If you lifted your fingers off the surface then there would be far too much power for the size of the pieces. So there was plenty of subtlety to Subbuteo. You had to learn to weight your passes and deliver them accurately. Was I good? Well, we had a little cup competition, and I did win it. And did I take that grin off George's face with this shot? I'm sure I did!

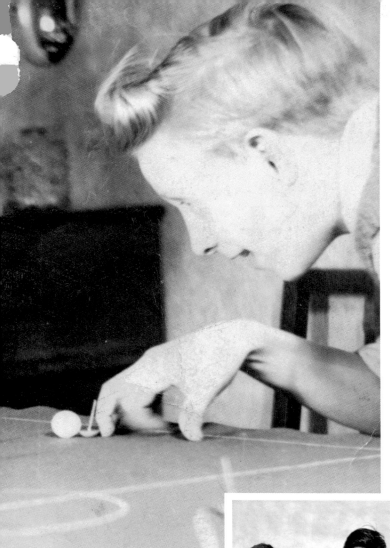

BELOW: The Powis secondary school in Aberdeen, round about 1954 – that's me second from the left on the front row. This must have been a formal picture, not an impromptu shot before a game, because I never wore my glasses to play. Another clue is that I've put in a bit of work on the hair!

Did I always have that competitive edge that I took into my career? Well, football *was* my life and I suppose I always did play as if my life depended on it. At the time we didn't have anything else. There was no money to buy proper kit, but there was a lamp-post and a jacket for goalposts, or maybe just a stone or a piece of wood, and so there was a game. We kicked the ball in the streets, on the way to school, between lessons, on the way home, before tea and then after tea until dark. Then I would go inside and play in the kitchen with a ball of wool attached to the clothes line. There was no TV, rarely any radio, perhaps the occasional comic if we were very lucky. So football dominated my day, dominated my whole life, and the whole thing was to win.

You might recognise a couple of the other faces here. The goalkeeper is John Ogston, who made a name for himself with Aberdeen before a brief stint with Liverpool, and next to me in the centre of the front row is my mate Gordon Low, who was with me at Huddersfield before giving long and distinguished service to Bristol City.

ABOVE: I was bursting with pride to wear the dark blue of Scotland at Under-15 level – you can hardly miss me in my specs on the right of the back row – even though I had to cover the shirt with my windcheater because I was only a squad member at this point.

The big, handsome devil with the ball at his feet is Willie Stevenson, who started at Ibrox but couldn't get in the Rangers team because of the prodigious talent of Jim Baxter. Eventually he went to Liverpool, where he played a big part in Bill Shankly's side rising to the top. Willie was a tremendous player, a lovely passer who completed a fine half-back line along with Gordon Milne and big Ron Yeats.

This was taken when we faced Northern Ireland at Windsor Park in Belfast, which was always a picturesque ground with the mountain in the background. Well, in Scotland we'd call it a hill . . .

ABOVE: Dad and Mum back home at 6 Printfield Terrace, Aberdeen, with a framed picture of me in my new Huddersfield kit on the sideboard behind them. I think they were proud of what I had managed to achieve, and I was pleased to be able to look after them with a few pounds. I was homesick for five or six years after leaving as a 15-year-old and stepping into what was, for me, a very strange new world. In those days it took 12 hours just to get to Huddersfield, travelling by train via York and Leeds. When I went down with my brothers, George and Johnny, it was one of my first times out of Scotland and the whole trip was an incredible eye-opener. We stayed at a boarding house and when we saw the breakfast – orange juice, bacon, egg and toast – we could only gasp. Back home it was a piece of toast and nothing more.

Dad was never a football fan, even when I did all right at the game. He was an out-and-out fisherman, who worked very hard, was away for long spells, and just liked his pint of beer when he had a moment to himself. To him, what I was doing was just another job. My parents were in their sixties at this point, and I always remember them as being fairly elderly. Unfortunately, I didn't really know my dad, which is something I do regret. He was at sea when I was a boy, so I saw him only at weekends, and then I was gone at 15.

CHAPTER 2

A TARTAN TERRIER

ABOVE: Bill Shankly leans over my shoulder, making sure I put my name in the right place on my first professional contract for Huddersfield in February 1957, with the club chairman and secretary looking on.

Shanks was always rasping away with his one-liners and he never changed. Football was his life and he was so enthusiastic that he made you want to play for him. He absolutely galvanised everybody around him. When I was on the groundstaff, after we'd done our work he'd have us playing five-a-side. He'd be against us and he'd be scoring the goals with total ruthlessness. We'd be thinking, 'What's going on? We're only fifteen', but he always wanted to win.

BILL SHANKLY:

Right from the start Denis stood out with his enthusiasm and will to win – nastiness, if you like. He would have died to have won. He would have kicked you to have won. He had a temper, and he was a terror – a bloody terror, with ability.

RIGHT: One of the happiest moments in the life of a professional footballer. The game is over, Huddersfield have obviously won or I wouldn't be smiling, I'm caked in mud and getting ready for a bath, while looking forward to a few well-earned beers with the lads. Saturday was the one night when we'd have a drink – there was never a game on a Sunday or Monday as there is today. We had trained hard all week, then battled through a game, and we needed that relaxation.

The state of my legs tells the story of how pitches were in the 1950s. Most of them were mudheaps from November onwards, but nobody complained because that was normal to us. Today everything has changed so drastically – the playing surface, the ball, the gear, the whole environment. There were no health drinks then. We just had a cup of tea before jumping into a communal bath in which the water would turn to a thick, brown goo within a couple of minutes.

The dressing room is always the heart of a club, a place of wicked fun most of the time, but also somewhere for the dispensing of home truths. It can be very hectic, but before a game I liked to stretch out on a bench and go to sleep. I didn't want to stuff my head full of tactics. The way I saw it, we were like gladiators waiting to meet the lions. We were going out to do battle. I didn't want to hear about the opposition, or to chat with them. For me the banter was after the game, never before it. That was time for concentrating on business. It's not always easy to nap in a busy dressing room, but all the guys knew what I was like and that I wouldn't be receptive to verbal approaches. That's a polite way of putting it!

ABOVE: I can recall this moment as clearly as if it were yesterday, which I guess is hardly surprising as I was scoring my first FA Cup goal at the tender age of 16. We were at home to the famous giant-killers Peterborough United, and although they were non-League at the time the joint was really hopping, with nearly 50,000 fans packed inside Leeds Road. Kevin McHale tore down the right touchline and slung in one of his typical teasing crosses, which I met on the volley from ten yards out and the ball just flew into the net. There aren't many better feelings than that for a kid, especially as we went on to win the game 3-1.

OPPOSITE TOP: I'm happy to identify myself as this likely lad without a hint of a squint, well groomed and ready for anything back in 1959. Soon after joining the Huddersfield groundstaff, I was called back to Aberdeen for an operation to get rid of my infuriating eyesight affliction, and that procedure changed my life completely. All of a sudden, for the first time in ten years, I had two straight eyes. It gave me more confidence on the field, because I no longer had to play with one eye closed and, crucially, I felt a lot better about facing the world in general. Suddenly I wasn't a bad-looking guy! I could look a girl straight in the eye. I only wish I looked like that now . . .

BELOW: A pretty typical winter scene at Leeds Road, Huddersfield, where we're shivering ahead of kick-off in an FA Cup tie with Burnley in February 1957. I don't want to bang on too much about the dreadful pitches in my time, but I do envy today's players the immaculate conditions they enjoy. This was a decent surface compared to some of the horrendous quagmires we experienced, but I was lucky to be an attacker. It was bad enough for all of us, but for defenders it was an absolute nightmare having to turn quickly in such treacherous conditions.

The fella freezing to my left is Dave Hickson, a big, brave battering-ram of a centre-forward who was nicknamed the Stormy Petrel because, just occasionally, he might lose his temper during a game. I could identify with him (I can't think why!), but having been in digs with him, I can vouch for the fact that he's a lovely man. Swinging his arms to keep warm in the background is Kevin McHale, another of my mates.

Sadly, we lost the game 2-1 and went out of the cup, which was particularly frustrating after struggling through two replays to beat Sheffield United in an earlier round.

ABOVE: Bill Shankly was a football evangelist and the players hung on every word he said. He didn't know anything about anything else apart from boxing, in which I wasn't interested, and films, especially the ones starring James Cagney. He did brilliant impersonations, and he was just like Cagney anyway. Look at his expression, his stance, even his hands; you could imagine Cagney just like that when he was saying, 'We got to look after those guys down in the Bronx . . .'

The beauty of Shanks, too, was that he really cared for his boys, knowing that we had just left home and were coming to terms with a new town or, in my case, a new country. He knew we needed feeding up, because we hadn't had a great deal of food since the war due to rationing in our childhoods, and he gave instructions to the woman in the café across the road from the ground to make sure we ate well.

Here the great man has the ball in his hands, preaching the gospel to, left to right, Harry Fearnley, Willie Davie, Kevin McHale, Dave Hickson, Ray Wilson, Les Massie, Jack Connor, myself, skipper Len Quested, Brian Gibson and Ronnie Simpson.

OPPOSITE: The High Priest of Leeds Road, to whom I owed everything for any early success I enjoyed – and when he left for Liverpool in December 1959 I thought I'd be going with him. Certainly, if I'd had an offer from Anfield at that point then I'd have accepted it, even though they were in the Second Division and, having had a taste of international football, I was raising my sights.

The funny thing is that the year before Shanks left for Merseyside we hammered Liverpool 5-0 and he was calling them the worst side in the world. Then he moved and suddenly he was describing them as the team of the future. It seemed a bit ironic, but the fact was he had this remarkable gift. He made people believe.

ABOVE: The training methods at Huddersfield were hardly the last word in sophistication, but certainly when Bill Shankly was in charge they were both effective and enjoyable. Here five of us are on our marks under the main stand at Leeds Road for a short, sharp sprint, exactly the sort of explosive bursts footballers need. Shanks came up with routines like this one, which we'd never had before, and usually they were fun, although he was a very tough taskmaster. He insisted that most of our fitness work was done with the ball and that was just what was needed. In those days, many clubs concentrated heavily on running around the track, which was deadly dull, and although it might have built stamina, it wasn't ideally tailored for the game.

Ready to spring into action here are, left to right, Derek Hawksworth, Kevin McHale, Jack Connor, myself and Ray Wilson (the future England World Cup winner).

ABOVE: I've always been one for getting back to my roots, and this was a close-season visit to the Laws' family home and my birthplace, 6 Printfield Terrace in Aberdeen, during the late 1950s. The two lads in the middle are Huddersfield team-mates, Gordon Low in the dark sweater and Jack Connor, while the other fella is a pal name of Billy Meldrum.

We lived on the ground floor of this three-storey tenement, which was built to last from granite, and it doesn't look a lot different today, apart from the windows. The street outside, where I learned to play football, has changed a bit, though. Now it's full of vehicles and industrial-size recycling bins, so kids can't play there as they did in my time, when there was only one car in the street. That's progress, I suppose.

LEFT: Football dieticians of the 21st century might be appalled at this meal of beef steak, tomatoes, fried onions, mashed potatoes and veg on the evening before a game, but I can assure you that to this unworldly 16-year-old in February 1957, it was nothing short of culinary heaven. Considering what I had been used to at home, where even a glass of orange juice was an unimagined luxury, it felt as if all my birthdays had come at once. So I was all in favour of Bill Shankly's master plan to build up the physique of this scrawny little lad from Aberdeen. Steak in Printfield Terrace? Not a chance. The only time we ever saw meat was an occasional serving of mince and tatties, and that was considered a treat.

I was never a particularly big eater compared to some of the lads, and I suppose I was lucky that I never put on weight no matter how many calories I took on board. When you consider that I was actually being paid to play football, something I loved with such a passion, you'll understand why I could hardly believe my good fortune. I couldn't think of anything better – this was top, top living.

BELOW LEFT: When Gordon Low, my old pal from Aberdeen, got married in 1960, he chose me as his best man, a decision that turned out to be a bit of a disaster. I didn't exactly cover myself in glory with my speech, but that wouldn't have surprised him, as public speaking was hardly my scene. After the reception, however, there was worse to come.

Having recently joined Manchester City I had bought my first car, and naturally enough volunteered to drive the happy couple to Huddersfield station, where they were due to catch a train to London for their three-day honeymoon. Very carefully I stowed the luggage in the boot of the car, but there had been a few drinks, and that minor detail went out of my head. Duly I dropped off Gordon and his bride, Brenda, and drove away with a girl of my own in tow – this was before I had met the lovely Diana, who was to become my wife – and I thought no more about the newlyweds.

Now, I can't recall how I was contacted, because mobile phones would have seemed like something out of science fiction half a century ago, but soon I received a message to say I'd driven off with the Lows' suitcase. They had no choice but to forgo the bright lights of London and book into a Huddersfield hotel for their wedding night, while I went very meekly and apologetically to drop off the missing item.

In my own defence, I must point out that they hadn't remembered their luggage, either, so you might say the blame should be shared 50:50, although I guess that, as best man, the buck stopped with me. I'm happy to say that Gordon didn't bear a grudge, and we remain good mates to this day.

ABOVE: Bill Shankly had turned Huddersfield into a decent side and we felt ready for anything as we faced the camera ahead of the 1959-60 campaign. He left for Liverpool in December and I joined Manchester City in the spring, but the lads managed to finish sixth in the old Second Division, not too far off the promotion pace. Back row, left to right: Brian Gibson, Gordon Low, Ray Wood, John Coddington, Bill McGarry and Ray Wilson. Front row: Kevin McHale, myself, Jack Connor, Les Massie and Derek Hawksworth.

OPPOSITE: Dominoes was a favourite pastime with most of the Huddersfield lads when we went out for our weekly drink together. Gordon Low and Jack Connor were our men to beat, but it was never really my game. Mind, I reckon I'd stand a chance against today's professional footballers. I don't think too many of them would even know the rules.

LES MASSIE:

Denis was full of life both on and off the pitch. He always loved a laugh and, as a pair of Aberdonians in digs together, we had plenty of fun. Mind, I didn't always think it was so funny when I was carrying him home from the pub, or when I was dropped – temporarily as it turned out – for him to make his debut as a 16-year-old.

ABOVE: I loved it when Huddersfield played in white shirts, because it reminded me of the great Real Madrid side of that era, that peerless combination featuring Alfredo di Stefano, Ferenc Puskas and Francisco Gento. They were the best club side I ever saw, and I fell utterly in love with them on the evening of 18 May 1960, when they defeated Eintracht Frankfurt 7-3 at Hampden Park with the most inspirational display imaginable to win the European Cup for the fifth season in succession.

What a contrast to the fare Scotland and England had served up at the old stadium some five weeks earlier when we had drawn 1-1 and the game had been utter garbage, including my own contribution. The pitch that day was terrible, but I knew we couldn't blame it when I thought about the magic Real Madrid had created so recently on that very same turf.

You might say all this has precious little to do with this shot of me shielding the ball from Leyton Orient's Dennis Sorrell at Brisbane Road in January 1960, but I'd contend that anything that conjures up beautiful images of di Stefano and company is welcome at any time.

CHAPTER 3

AN ANGLO IN DARK BLUE

ABOVE: I'm young and fit and ready for action, the sun is shining brightly and I have a Scotland shirt on my back. Who could ask for more?

ABOVE: Locked in combat with John Charles when Wales were the visitors to Hampden Park in November 1959. It was always going to be an arduous physical battle against Big John because of his size, but at least you could be certain of a scrupulously fair contest. Here I'm turning away from him with the ball, but there was no way he would have tried to bring me down.

John was one of the finest footballers who ever lived, being equally at home in central defence or leading the attack. In the late 1950s he was the best header of a ball anywhere in the world, but his all-round game was brilliant, too. Sadly, British fans missed his peak, because it was spent in Italy with Juventus during an era before the blanket TV coverage of top European

matches, and also injury forced him out of Wales' World Cup quarter-final against Brazil in 1958 when he would have been in the spotlight. Some said he might have achieved even greater things had he been more ruthless, but that was never John's way. There wasn't a nasty bone in his body or a malicious thought in his head. He was known as the Gentle Giant, and never has a nickname been more appropriate.

This is my sixth game for Scotland and I was still looking for my second goal. The first had come on my debut, also against Wales but at Ninian Park, and had been a complete fluke – a clearance from keeper Jack Kelsey whacking me on the back of the head and ending up in the net.

LEFT: The atmosphere was convivial in the Scotland camp under the man who was both my first full-time international boss and my first Huddersfield manager, Andy Beattie (left). He was a really nice guy, very friendly and courteous, but he wasn't one to inspire a team, or scare the living daylights out of his players if necessary, like, say, Bill Shankly, his successor at Leeds Road.

Here Andy's joking with his forward line – left to right, John White (inside-right), Graham Leggat (right-wing), Bertie Auld (left-wing), Ian St John (centre-forward) and myself (inside-left) – ahead of our 1-1 draw with Wales at Hampden Park in November 1959. Graham, who hailed from my home town of Aberdeen, was a dashing attacker down the right flank and he scored plenty of goals, including the one in this match.

IAN ST JOHN:

The Lawman was a mickey-taker, always up to some nonsense, and as he's the only one here with a straight face I'd guess that he was waiting to deliver a wicked punchline. Andy was a decent man, but with Bill Shankly at the helm we might have won anything. Scotland had some of the best players in the world at the time, and Denis was one of them.

LEFT: One of the joys of international duty was meeting up with the other Scottish lads, such as John White, who I'm greeting here as we gather for training ahead of our game with the Netherlands in Amsterdam in May 1959. At the time, a few months before his transfer from Falkirk to Tottenham Hotspur, John was maybe a wee bit shy, just as I was when pitched into a squad full of household names.

Soon enough, though, he emerged as a delightful personality with a tremendous sense of fun. Meanwhile, there was never any doubt that he was a fantastic footballer with limitless potential, which only served to emphasise the stark tragedy of his death, struck by lightning on a golf course when he was only 24 and nowhere near his prime. I was on holiday in Scotland in July 1964 when I heard he'd been killed, and I just couldn't believe my ears. It was utterly devastating.

I was in awe of John's astonishing command of a football. He used to put down a two-bob (10p) coin, wedge it on its side in the grass and then chip a ball at it from 20 yards away, knocking it down every time. If you think that's easy, just try it for yourself.

There was nothing of him physically, he was as thin as a stick, but if he had lived he would have become one of the best Scotland players of all time. His passing was sublime, he could score goals and his movement was uncanny. He was dubbed 'The Ghost' because he would appear in space apparently from nowhere, invariably when you were desperate for someone to pass to, and he had remarkable stamina. As for keepy-uppy, I could never manage more than about ten, but John could keep it going all morning.

ABOVE: Edinburgh Castle looms in the background as three young men about town – John White (left), Dave Mackay (centre) and myself – contemplate an evening out. I'm bound to say that I'm looking the smoothest, in my Italian suit, though it might be stretching a point to say they're gazing at me in admiration.

Dave was a magnificent player and a fantastic man. After international games in Glasgow we didn't have to return to club training until the Friday and usually I would go through to his home town of Edinburgh for a night out with him – and, believe me, a night out with Dave Mackay was invariably one to remember.

ABOVE: There aren't words to describe my pride to be playing for Scotland against England at Hampden Park in front of 130,000 supporters in my first clash with the 'Auld Enemy' at senior level. Just feast your eyes on the awesome scene – the sunshine and shadows on a crisp spring afternoon, the vivid contrast of the white and dark blue shirts, the rich golden leather ball, the cut and thrust of furious action, that vast bank of howling humanity in the background. Aah, I was in paradise.

To me Scotland against England was the supreme sporting spectacle, every detail of which was etched indelibly on to the minds of boys who dreamed of nothing but football. To actually play in it was more than I could ever have asked and even the unfortunate fact that this particular 1-1 draw in April 1960 was a pretty dire football match could not ruin the occasion for me.

What must it have been like for the England lads to face that roaring multitude? Some must have been intimidated, although Bobby Charlton always loved it. Of course, the Scottish fans loved him, too, though that same warmth was not extended to most of his team-mates!

Here I'm about to shoot for goal with my left foot, England skipper Ronnie Clayton is attempting to block me and Bill Slater is poised to snap up any rebound. For the record I didn't score. Our goal was contributed by Graham Leggat and Bobby equalised from the penalty spot.

OPPOSITE: Put it there, my Lord Provost of Glasgow. I'm introduced to the holder of that lofty office, one Myer Galpern, before we face England at Hampden Park in April 1960. To my right is Alex Young, next to him is his Hearts team-mate John Cumming and you can just make out the distinctive wavy red hair of skipper Bobby Evans of Celtic, who was ushering the dignitary along the line of players.

Alex was a gloriously gifted centre-forward blessed with beautifully subtle ball skills and it's remarkable to reflect that he collected only eight caps. True, there was no shortage of exceptional rivals, notably Ian St John, vying for the No 9 shirt, but still I think Alex could consider himself a bit unfortunate.

ABOVE: When football was truly the people's game and Glaswegians could watch the Scotland team training from their front-room windows. In fact, from the top storey of the tenements in the background, I wouldn't be surprised if the residents could catch a glimpse of the game at Hampden Park, which was very close. Here we're preparing for the visit of Northern Ireland in November 1960 and were about to be put through our paces at Lesser Hampden, the training pitch in the shadow of the main ground. Looking typically dapper on the left of the back row is the manager, Ian McColl, who wasn't as famous as fellow Scots Matt Busby or Bill Shankly, but he was a good man and did a tremendously efficient job for his country during the first half of the 1960s. Also in the back row, left to right, are Duncan MacKay, Dave Mackay, Jackie Plenderleith, Lawrie Leslie, Jim Baxter, Eric Caldow, Jimmy Millar and trainer Dawson Walker. At the front are George Herd, myself, Alex Young, Ralph Brand and Davie Wilson

ABOVE: You know, it's a curious thing, but I can't recall very much at all about Scotland's 9-3 defeat by England at Wembley in April 1961. They tell me it happened, they even insist that I played, but somehow the details escape me . . .

Hang on, though. Delving into the darkest corners of my memory, it comes back to me that we went three down, then fought back to 3-2 and at that stage we had England going. But then we conceded a sloppy fourth and the roof fell in. Without crucifying the poor guy, it's fair to say that our keeper, Frank Haffey, didn't have his best day. In the end it was comfortably Scotland's blackest footballing hour. It was bad enough to perform like that at Wembley, but if it had been Hampden we'd never have got off the pitch. We'd have been slaughtered!

Before the match, in blissful ignorance of the nightmare in store, skipper Eric Caldow introduces me to the Duke of Edinburgh. That's Johnny MacLeod on my right and Ian St John on my left.

OPPOSITE TOP: The Saint (No 9) and myself look on in frustration as England keeper Ron Springett collects a cross.

IAN ST JOHN:

I don't know why Denis has brought up such a painful subject. I've been trying to forget it for half a century, and now I'm feeling the pain all over again. After the game there was a banquet and we were so distraught all we could do was to get as much alcohol as possible down our necks to erase the memory. I thought I'd succeeded – until now!

BELOW: The entire Welsh defence, including John Charles (left) and Stuart Williams (foreground), appear convinced that I'm offside in this typically wholehearted encounter at Ninian Park in October 1962. I loved playing there, under the famous advertisement for Captain Morgan rum, because the atmosphere was always fantastic and, whimsical though it might seem today, I believe there might have been something in the violently clashing colours of our shirts, the deep red and the dark blue, that somehow stirred the blood.

Welsh fans had a passion not unlike the Scots and the Irish. We were all small Celtic nations who wore our hearts on our sleeves and who felt we had to do something special to beat England. We all had far fewer players to choose from, but in recent years we had both produced some fantastic performers. In Wales' case there were John and Mel Charles, Cliffie Jones, Ivor and Len Allchurch – the list runs on. At the time we took it for granted that our countries would always nurture wonderful footballers – little did we dream of the famine to come. Now I'm sad to say that, thanks to the dearth of home-grown lads in the Premier League, England are likely to face a similar decline.

For the record, Scotland won this game 3-2, with our goals coming from Willie Henderson, Eric Caldow and myself.

OPPOSITE: It's pretty obvious from the grins on the faces of Willie Henderson and myself, as we leave the Hampden pitch after facing Northern Ireland in November 1962, that we have won the match. In fact, the pair of us were walking on air as, between us, we had scored all the goals in our 5-1 victory. I had managed four of them myself – it was one of those games in which everything you hit goes in. You don't expect to score four in an international, but it can happen, and I was lucky enough to do it again on the same turf a year later against Norway.

Wee Willie was a charismatic fella who liked to have fun, and a marvellous player. Alex Scott was a terrific right-winger, too, but he lost his Scotland place to Willie, whose explosive emergence in the early 1960s made it easy for Rangers to sell Alex to Everton. There wasn't much of Willie, but he was tough, brave and he scored goals.

Strolling off behind us is our skipper, Eric Caldow, a steady left-back for Rangers and Scotland for many seasons, and a gentleman. Sadly, he was never the same after breaking his leg against England at Wembley in 1963.

BELOW: Life was sweet that night at Hampden, though the Irish defenders might have begged to differ. Here I'm celebrating Willie Henderson's goal, while keeper Bobby Irvine and centre-half Sammy Hatton can be forgiven for looking a trifle glum.

CHAPTER 4

BIG CITY

ABOVE: When I moved to Manchester City as a £55,000 British record signing in March 1960, I needed a mentor on and off the pitch, and that man turned out to be the club skipper, Ken Barnes, who sized me up for the No 8 shirt at our first meeting.

Switching from Huddersfield to Manchester felt like leaving a village for a huge, sprawling city, and I was still only a boy of 20. So Ken, with all his experience of the game and life in general, was perfect for me. He showed me around the place, took me to the right restaurants and nightclubs, added a few words to my vocabulary – you might call them Birmingham slang – and generally looked after me. As a result we became lifelong friends, and I was devastated when he died in July 2010, though I could rejoice in the reflection that he had packed an enormous amount into his 81 years on the planet. Certainly Ken was an excellent player, a creative wing-half who loved to push up into attack, as I recalled from watching him in the FA Cup finals of 1955 and 1956.

At the time of my transfer, I had received a solid approach from Arsenal, Everton were said to be interested, as was Shanks at Liverpool, so I thought they might come in for me at some point. But I was more than happy to be joining City, where the manager was Les McDowall, a calm, dignified, pipe-smoking Scot. Now who does that put you in mind of?

KEN BARNES:

Bloody hell! What a player he was! He didn't look much at first viewing. A skinny little bugger, he was. He looked like a stiff breeze would blow him over. Talk about appearances being deceptive – he was the perfect inside-forward. He could do everything. He was like lightning, he grafted, he could lick people, he scored goals – wonderful, absolutely top class.

As a striker he was one of the best I've ever seen and I've seen a few. But I always tell anyone who'll listen that he had so much more to his game than goals. As a youngster he reminded me of Peter Doherty and I can't pay him a bigger compliment than that. You couldn't take your eyes off him.

Funnily enough, he could be a quiet laddie off the field, but on it the bugger looked like he owned the bloody place. He had a bit of devil about him – no one took liberties with Denis.

ABOVE: I was dreaming of footballing fulfilment, not filling my pockets, when I agreed to enlist with Manchester City. There was no question of huge financial inducements, because the maximum wage rule was still in force. All I wanted was to be part of this big club with bags of tradition and a fine team in which I could pit myself against the top players of the day. The way it worked out, City were a side in decline and that was disappointing, although I really enjoyed my season and a bit at Maine Road. They still had some tremendous players and colourful characters – the likes of Ken Barnes, keeper Bert Trautmann and clever inside-forward George Hannah – but as a combination we couldn't rise above mid-table mediocrity. As for my fee, it was just something I had to live with. Having cost more money than anyone else, I realised there were sky-high expectations and I wanted to meet them.

Lining up at the start of the 1960-61 campaign are, back row left to right: Bert Lister, George Hannah, Cliff Sear, Bert Trautmann, Barry Betts, Jackie Plenderleith, Alan Oakes. Front row: Colin Barlow, Joe Hayes, Ken Barnes, myself, Clive Colbridge.

LEFT: What a joy it was to be young and healthy with the world at your feet. As I celebrated my 21st birthday in February 1961 at my digs in Withington, Manchester, there wasn't a cloud on my horizon. Yet though I was happy enough with life at Manchester City, I was very ambitious, too. In all honesty, as I've said, they were not a great side at the time, and I must admit that the thought of seeking fame and fortune in the Italian sun was beginning to take shape.

BELOW: I was proud to wear City's lovely crisp pale blue shirt with the big white V-neck. The old strips were beautiful, absolutely different class, and with fans all over the country knowing every team's colours, they really meant something. But, like everything else in this world, football strips are not immune to change. I understand that clubs need sponsorship to be viable in the modern world, but I do feel that kits are cheapened by all the endless logos that are plastered over them today.

Here I'm kicking in before a game at Maine Road in 1960-61, with the dear old Platt Lane stand in the background.

ABOVE: Two new boys at one game constituted a gift for the photographers, who set up this snap of Freddie Goodwin and myself at Elland Road in March 1960. I was making my debut for City, following my record-breaking transfer from Huddersfield, and Freddie was playing his first game for Leeds, having just arrived from Manchester United. As luck would have it, we were in direct opposition, with Freddie at left-half marking me at inside-right. I was delighted to mark my first City appearance with a goal, but he had the last laugh because Leeds won 4-3. That day, too, a red-headed Scottish youngster by the name of Billy Bremner was on the scoresheet for the home team. Our paths would cross again.

It felt strange to be decked out in one of City's less familiar change strips, which consisted of gold shirts with maroon facings and black shorts. The only thing I didn't like about it was the short sleeves. I much preferred long ones, because I could clutch them with my fingers and there was more to wipe my nose on!

ABOVE: I suppose it's more than a little bit ironic that the contest for which I'm best remembered during my first spell with Manchester City is one in which I scored six goals, but only one of them counted – and we lost!

It was a fourth-round FA Cup tie at Luton in January 1961, the rain fell in torrents and the pitch was horrendous – an absolute quagmire. It was a strange match because Luton went two up with a couple of early efforts by Alec Ashworth, but then I managed a hat-trick before half time, this diving header being my second. By 67 minutes we had scored three more, two of them were mine and one was from Joe Hayes, though I was credited with it at first, but actually I never got a touch on his shot. But by then we were peering through a wall of water, it was impossible to move the ball about and the referee had no alternative but to call it off.

Naturally, it was hugely frustrating to have all those goals chalked off, and I could understand the City fans who had travelled to Kenilworth Road being really fed up, but it's a game and you just have to get on with it. The really disappointing thing was losing the re-match 3-1, and it was no consolation at all that I got our only goal.

OPPOSITE: Now that's what I call a rueful expression – and I look pretty cheesed off, too. The mutt was my landlady's, but I can't recall its name. Normally I don't like dogs, and I don't have anything to do with them, but I made an exception for the photographer after the Luton defeat. In fact, I was perfectly cheerful really and this was a terrific bit of acting. Mind you, it was probably the 50th take and I reckon the hound was sedated for me to get that close to him!

I consoled myself by thinking I was young enough to get another chance of reaching an FA Cup final and, sure enough, I did only two years later, even though by then I was playing for the other Manchester side. For a long time, until I was overtaken by Ian Rush, I was the FA Cup's record scorer with 40 goals, which of course didn't include that big haul at Kenilworth Road. But while you're still playing, all that matters is winning the game, and you're not bothered about records. I think it's more disappointing as you get older and look back when records go.

ABOVE: Am I as hacked off as I look after reading the report of the first game at Luton? Not really. I was hamming it up for the newspapers while getting my feet up back at my digs. I *was* knackered, though. Running around with mud up to our ankles was incredibly hard work.

CHAPTER 5

TUMULT IN TURIN

ABOVE: It wasn't the most difficult chance in the world, but scoring a goal in front of the massed legions of the San Siro was more than a little bit special for a 20-year-old who until recently had been plying his trade in the rather more humble surroundings of Leeds Road. I was playing for the Football League against the Italian League, and although we lost 4-2, I must have done something to attract the Italians' attention, because it wasn't too long after this game in November 1960 that whispers about a move to the land of the *lire* began to circulate.

The atmosphere in Milan was incredible. I loved it and it was one of the main reasons I accepted the transfer to Italy some six months later. The stands tower above you; it feels as though the fans are right on top of you, and they all have a fantastic view of the action. It was all very exhilarating and I wanted more.

As for this game, it was a great honour to play with the likes of England star Johnny Haynes (left) and Irishman Peter McParland (behind me). For the spindly little lad from Aberdeen to be in such company was truly amazing.

OPPOSITE: Two young men of the world on the adventure of a lifetime. Joe Baker and I had moved together to Torino – my fee was £110,000 – in the summer of 1961 and sometimes I had to pinch myself to believe what was happening. We were both from working-class families, we had never travelled any-where and now here we were jetting all over the place.

Just look at Joe, such a handsome, fun-loving lad – utterly irrepressible and fantastically entertaining company. We were both single and the *dolce vita* beckoned. There was so much to enjoy – the food, the wine, the nightclubs, the clothes, although I have absolutely no idea why we're wearing identical coats here. I admit that, looking back, it might have been a mistake for the two of us to be transferred together. Because we had each other, we didn't become as integrated into Italian life and culture as we might have done had we been solo.

Of course, it wasn't all milk and honey. Italy is always portrayed as sunny, but Turin is in the north and often it could be very cold. The paparazzi, too, could be a pain in the bum, but the worst aspect was the football, which was ridiculously defensive and, in my opinion, joyless.

Joe Baker could see the funny side of anything, even after a car crash in which we were lucky to escape with our lives. At first I'd done the driving in Italy, but then Joe bought an Alfa Romeo and we came to grief within a few miles of his taking possession. With Joe at the wheel we were going the wrong way round a roundabout when we clipped a kerb and the car did a couple of somersaults. Joe was thrown out and I was jerked sideways into his seat, while in the space which I'd vacated the roof had been crushed flush with the dashboard.

ABOVE: If I'd been wearing a safety belt I'd have been killed. As it was I was virtually unscathed, as was my brother Joe, who'd been travelling in the back. Poor Joe Baker, though, suffered hideous head injuries and was in a coma for weeks before a brilliant surgeon put his face back together.

ABOVE: Here the healing process is well under way, and once again we were fooling around for the cameras. Joe loved life so much and lived it to the full. I was devastated when he died, tragically prematurely, of a heart attack in 2003.

ABOVE: If I look like a rank novice when confronted by this bowl of spaghetti soon after moving to Turin in the summer of 1961, then it's hardly surprising. After all, in those days most people in Britain had precious little experience of Italian cuisine. Luckily for me, I had a perfect teacher in my agent and friend, Gigi Peronace, a fantastic man who introduced me to a whole new way of living.

Sure, it took me a little while to master the technique of wrapping the spaghetti around the spoon, but overall I think I was a pretty quick learner. Before long I was positively embracing the different culture. I loved the clothes and the food, and in no time at all a typical pint-of-lager lad from Aberdeen was turned on to wine. As a result, when I returned to England in 1962 and started asking for Pinot Noir or Chianti, everyone looked at me as if I was mad.

As for the spaghetti, I've got a shocking admission to make. These days I cut it up – not so messy, no splashing around, altogether more practical for a fellow my age!

LEFT: Duel in the sun. The Inter Milan right-back makes a clearance from under my nose during Torino's visit to the San Siro one sweltering afternoon in September 1961. I was lurking in the hope of a slip-up, but defensive mistakes were few and far between in that league. Although my year in Turin hardened me and improved my game, I have to admit I wasn't enamoured of the style of football, which basically involved Joe Baker and me operating on our own in front of a massed rearguard. It seemed that whoever got a goal won the game, because at 1-0 every team wanted to shut up shop. In the circumstances, I was pleased to hit the target ten times in 27 league games for Torino, but it wasn't the way I had been brought up to play.

I did adore our shirts, though. They were a beautiful rich maroon in colour as you can see in the team picture on the opposite page.

OPPOSITE: The calm before the storm – exchanging a few words with the defensive wing-half Mario David ahead of an encounter with AC Milan at the San Siro. The Italian international liked a tackle, seeing his job mainly as winning the ball and then giving it to a more creative colleague, frequently the gifted play-maker Gianni Rivera. It is never easy to play against an opponent who is both tough and intelligent, and it didn't surprise me when David went on to a career in coaching.

ABOVE: What I needed when I arrived in Turin was an Italian equivalent of Ken Barnes, who had looked after me so well in my early days with Manchester City, and that was exactly what I got in the form of Enzo Bearzot, seen here on the left of the back row. He was the skipper and a veteran, highly accomplished player, just the man to take Joe and me under his wing. I shall always be grateful to him for making us feel at home. Enzo was a strong character and I wasn't surprised when he became such a successful manager, leading Italy to World Cup glory in 1982.

Joe and I got on well with our team-mates, who seemed to relish having two young foreigners in their midst, a pair of strikers who brought something different to the team. Most of the guys didn't speak English and the few Italian words they taught us turned out to be dirty ones, which is typical of footballers' banter the world over.

In this group, that's me on the left of the front row, while Joe is standing third from the right.

A study in sheer charisma – and I'm not talking about Joe Baker (left), myself or Gerry Hitchens (right) as the Italian League party waits for the journey to Glasgow to face the Scottish League in November 1961. Big John Charles had some extra special quality that drew the eye no matter what he was doing, and yet there wasn't the slightest hint of conceit about him. When Joe and I joined Torino he was playing for our local rivals, Juventus, and was worshipped like a god. But he turned out to be a lovely, laid-back fella who took us under his wing and made life so much easier for two kids in a foreign land.

Even on the field he was a total gent. When we beat Juventus on their own ground, an event not far removed from the end of the world for their fanatical supporters, he was the first to congratulate us and wish us all the best for the next game. Sad to say, they don't make 'em like John Charles any more.

LEFT: It felt more than a little surreal to train at Little Hampden, in the shadow of Scotland's national stadium, with the word 'Italia' emblazoned on my chest and with two Englishmen and a Welshman as team-mates. I was in town along with my fellow British 'exiles', left to right, Gerry Hitchens of Internazionale, John Charles of Juventus and my Torino team-mate Joe Baker, to represent the Italian League against the Scottish League in November 1961.

We drew 1-1 with Gerry, the former Aston Villa man, scoring for us and Rangers' Ralph Brand replying for the Scots. It seemed strange to be facing international pals like Paddy Crerand, Jim Baxter, Davie Wilson and Eric Caldow, but it was such a phenomenal privilege to be photographed alongside Big John. He was 'The King', the top man, and compared to him the rest of us were boys, still learning about the game.

Looking at this picture now, it's spooky to realise that I'm the only one of us left alive. Believe me, that's not an easy concept to grasp.

OPPOSITE: I did love the clobber in Italy, and certainly I relished slipping into a sharp suit like this and striking a pose for the camera in 1961. In the past, everybody had worn a blue or a white shirt, but suddenly in the early 1960s pinks and yellows and all sorts of new shades were breaking out all over in Turin. Carnaby Street had not yet taken off and we were well ahead of the London game, right at the cutting edge of international style. If we'd really been into fashion, Joe Baker and I could have made one hell of a splash in gear that nobody back home could ever have imagined.

When I returned to Britain in 1962 to join Manchester United, I had so many wonderful clothes but I never wore them. Then Carnaby Street really got going in mid-decade and I was able to bring it all back out, staggering the rest of the lads at Old Trafford. Looking back, maybe I should have worn it all along – then I would have been trendier than George Best!

CHAPTER 6

NEW DAWN AT OLD TRAFFORD

ABOVE: I'm looking a wee bit cocky as I relax in an armchair in Matt Busby's office as the formalities of my £115,000 move from Torino to Manchester United are completed in July 1962. In fact, that jaunty demeanour masks an overwhelming feeling of relief that the deal had finally gone through after weeks of uncertainty. A transfer to the fierce local rivals Juventus had been mooted and I was placed under severe pressure to accept the move. It was even threatened that I would never play again unless I joined Juve, but I went home to Aberdeen, banking on the certainty that Torino wouldn't throw away a six-figure fee. Sure enough, it wasn't long before I got the call to Manchester and I could breathe easily again.

I had been anxious because Torino had messed United around in earlier negotiations, and I was afraid that Matt Busby might not come back. But he knew I wasn't enjoying Italy any more, he was still rebuilding in the wake of the Munich disaster and so I reckoned I still had a great chance of becoming a United player.

The fellow signing the transfer forms is United secretary Les Olive, while standing behind him are, left to right, my agent Gigi Peronace (who was also acting for Torino), Matt Busby and his deputy Jimmy Murphy. Amazingly, none of them commented on my socks.

ABOVE: 'Got you at last, son!' That's the gist of Matt Busby's words after I had signed on the dotted line, and from the look of our grins we were both pretty pleased with the deal. I felt I knew him pretty well already, having seen him on and off since I was a 16-year-old in Scotland's youth team. Back then he had offered to take me from Huddersfield for £10,000, at the time a huge amount of dosh for an unproved kid, but his pal Bill Shankly wasn't having any of that.

Now I was overjoyed to be working for someone I trusted and respected, and delighted to be back in Manchester where I had loads of friends. Also, it was important that I had been bought to play attacking football, the sort I loved. Unknown to me at the time, though, the type of game I had played under difficult and unfamiliar conditions in Italy had done me a great deal of good. It had given me an extra dimension, made me a more rounded player. With Torino, I had been constantly marked by two defenders. Now, in the much more open English game, it felt by comparison that I wasn't being marked at all. I was only 22, and the manager saw me as one of the building blocks of a new Old Trafford generation. I felt I had become part of something special at Old Trafford – and I was right.

ABOVE: Did the red shirt fit? You bet it did. I was always sensitive to the type of kit I played in and this felt perfect, complete with the long sleeves I always preferred. Far more handy than a handkerchief!

MATT BUSBY:

Denis was the most expensive signing I ever made. But in terms of sheer achievement, he turned out to be the cheapest. He was the most thrilling player in the game, the quickest thinker on the pitch I ever saw, and the greatest man in the penalty box. Nobody else scored so many miracle goals. When a chance was on for him, or a half-chance, or a quarter-chance, or a chance that was no sort of chance at all for anybody else but him, he would have it in the net with such power and acrobatic agility that colleagues and opponents alike could only stand and gasp.

JIMMY MURPHY:

If you had to send somebody out to score a goal to save your life, there could be only one man – the Lawman.

ABOVE: This was the first time I sat down to be photographed with my new Manchester United team-mates, at our Stretford training ground in the summer of 1962. Matt Busby had not yet finished his post-Munich reconstruction job, but there were plenty of strong characters in the squad, and I knew Old Trafford was the place to be.

There were some terrific youngsters, notably a boy from Belfast – no, not that one, I'll get to him later! This was a richly talented wing-half called Jimmy Nicholson. He looked set for an incredible career, and he did have a decent one, mainly with my old club Huddersfield, but it's fair to say he never quite hit the heights expected of him. I don't know why, perhaps it had something to do with being dubbed 'the new Duncan Edwards'. Saddling young boys with such pressure is appallingly unfair, but the media do it all the time.

Left to right, back row: Maurice Setters, Jimmy Nicholson, David Gaskell, Shay Brennan, Mark Pearson, Noel Cantwell (captain). Middle row: Bill Foulkes, Sammy McMillan, Tony Dunne, Nobby Stiles, Nobby Lawton. Front row: Johnny Giles, Albert Quixall, David Herd, myself, Bobby Charlton.

BILL FOULKES:

When Denis walked in to Old Trafford in the summer of 1962, he galvanised the place. We were already a pretty good team with some excellent players, but it was Denis who provided that vital spark that could make all the difference against high-quality opponents. Of course, he was blessed with fabulous skills, but also he was phenomenally brave; he was one of the most enthusiastic individuals I had ever met and there was always a touch of stardust about him. I think my wife, Teresa, summed up his appeal perfectly when she said: 'The game always seemed so much more exciting when Denis was playing.' I know he cost a king's ransom, but he was worth every last penny. He's a smashing lad, too. I'm very proud to have been associated with Denis Law.

ABOVE: It was reassuring to know that I'd be linking up with a world-class performer in Bobby Charlton, who I knew quite a bit about through facing him at international level. The beauty of playing with a top footballer is that it's easy. The better the man alongside you, the simpler it is for you to express yourself. In those days, he was lining up on the left wing, a position he didn't particularly relish but one in which he excelled. He was a fabulous striker of the ball, a tireless runner and a tremendous crosser who always seemed able to find me at the near post. When he had the ball, I knew exactly where to run and we had an instinctive understanding, which was maybe like the one Ryan Giggs and Paul Scholes enjoy today.

Of course, Bobby went on to reach his full potential in central midfield alongside Paddy Crerand, who was soon to join the club.

BOBBY CHARLTON:

When Matt Busby signed Denis I couldn't have been happier because I knew he was a tremendous player, one of the best I'd ever seen. As it turned out, I wasn't even beginning to do him justice. He hit Old Trafford like a flash of lightning, breathing new life into the team with his fearlessness, his unshakeable self-belief and his astonishing ability to score sensational goals out of nothing. Now United were radiating confidence again and so much of that was down to Denis.

LEFT: At Brisbane Road in the autumn of 1962, looking confident and ready for the fray, eager for the glory to kick off. In fact, I had to be patient. That day we lost 1-0 to newly promoted Leyton Orient and by season's end we had only narrowly avoided being relegated to the Second Division. Quite definitely, that had not been in the script, but still I believed we had the nucleus of an exciting side and that it was just a question of getting in a few more quality players. Paddy Crerand, for instance. For some reason that winter's Big Freeze seemed to disrupt us more than most, but success in the FA Cup helped us to turn a corner, after which we never looked back.

I'm astonished by my neatness here, with my shirt tucked tidily into my shorts. I preferred to leave it hanging free, which I found more comfortable. Lots of managers might tell you to smarten up, but once I was on the field Matt Busby had no choice. Often, though, I'd tuck the shirt in while walking up the tunnel at half time to avoid unnecessary arguments. George was the same – we were the scruffy ones, while Bobby used to conform.

LEFT: I like the hats. Mind you the fancy headgear didn't help Paddy Crerand (centre) and Maurice Setters (right) with their golf. They were garbage, these two. They were midfield players used to kicking people, and they could batter the ball, right enough, but they had no finesse whatsoever. But let's be fair, they were good lads to have on your side, and two of my best friends at the time.

What can I say about Paddy? You might call him a forthright individual (!) and unquestionably he was a tremendous footballer whom I had recommended enthusiastically to our fellow Scot, Matt Busby. True, Crerand didn't have quite the comprehensive range of attributes that Jim Baxter could boast, but there weren't many finer distributors of the ball than Paddy. These days the media churn out exhaustive statistics about each player's passes and I'm sure if they'd been around in his day, Paddy would have been peerless.

Maurice was a hard man on the pitch, a motivator, and he was a tough guy on the golf course, too. You had to make sure you were behind him when he was hitting the ball – but I couldn't blame him if he said the same thing about Paddy and me.

PADDY CRERAND:

I never wear a hat. This must have been for a bet. Denis was a decent golfer who could hit the ball a mile, though the direction could vary a bit. As for Maurice, he played golf the way he played football – viciously!

LEFT: I'm straining every sinew to prevent United from losing a third game on the belt in September 1962, but to no avail. It looks as though I might have evaded the challenge of Sheffield Wednesday goalkeeper Ron Springett, but I failed to score and we went down 1-0, thus continuing our disappointing start to the campaign. Ron was England's No 1 before Gordon Banks, and although he wasn't the tallest, he was always a difficult man to beat.

Looking on is wing-half Tony Kay, a tough and talented performer who went on to win a title medal with Everton that season but who threw everything away through his part in the infamous football bribes scandal. His punishment was effectively a lifelong suspension from the game, just as he had got into the England team. It seemed all the more tragic because he made only a tiny amount of money from his misdemeanour, which he committed during his Wednesday days, yet he had ruined a richly promising career and brought shame on his family. What a waste!

ABOVE: There weren't too many more daunting physical chal-
lenges in English football than facing Tony Knapp and the
rest of an abrasively combative Southampton defence on a
lumpy mudheap, but with a place at Wembley as the prize, I
was delighted to have the opportunity at Villa Park in the late
spring of 1963. The Saints – an ironic nickname if ever I
heard one – were in the Second Division at the time, but they
were a decent side and had nothing to lose in this FA Cup
semi-final showdown. At least we weren't at The Dell, where
they were a truly formidable proposition with their fans so
near to a tightly enclosed pitch. It reminded me of Palermo in
Sicily, where if you fell into the crowd you feared you might
not come out again.

As for United, we were enduring a disastrous time in the
league, still battling to avoid the drop, so we were desperate to
succeed in the knockout competition. Here Knapp has beaten
me to the ball in what was a relentlessly tense encounter that
had both sets of fans on edge till the final whistle. Just look at
that crowd, open to the sky and towering behind the goal like
a range of hills. In these safety-conscious days, such vast banks
of seething humanity are a thing of the past.

ABOVE: It always seemed likely that a single goal would settle this dour struggle with Southampton, and luckily it fell to me to score it. The ball came into a crowded six-yard box, there was an almighty scramble and I managed to stick out a leg to prod it over the line. Not pretty, but absolutely priceless, immensely significant for United at that time. Had we gone out in the semi-final to a Second Division club, then the mood would have darkened at Old Trafford and we might not have escaped from relegation, which would have been unthinkable.

As it was, we had made it to the final in my first season back in England, and we went on to an uplifting afternoon in the Wembley sunshine, which proved to be a glorious watershed for the team. It was a situation that was mirrored nearly 30 years later when Alex Ferguson led United to the FA Cup final in 1990 after floundering in the league. Then, as for us in the 1960s, a glittering future was beckoning.

THE FOOTBALL ASSOCIATION CHALLENGE CUP COMPETITION

THE FOOTBALL ASSOCIATION CENTENARY YEAR

FINAL TIE

LEICESTER CITY

v

MANCHESTER UNITED

OFFICIAL PROGRAMME · ONE SHILLING

WEMBLEY

EMPIRE STADIUM

SATURDAY, MAY 25th · Kick-off 3 p.m.

ABOVE: After the chronic winter we'd endured, playing on the beautifully smooth green turf at a sun-drenched Wembley seemed like heaven. Mind, it was stiflingly hot that day and if we'd had to chase the game in the FA Cup final against Leicester it would not have been easy. Fortunately, I managed to score the first goal after half an hour, which gave us a bit of breathing space.

There didn't seem to be any danger as Gordon Banks threw the ball in the direction of my Scottish international team-mate Davie Gibson. But our recent signing Paddy Crerand spotted the intention and beat Gibson to the ball, then speared one of his beautiful trademark passes to me on the other side of the box. It came behind me and I had to spin, and then hit a lucky shot into the far corner. It was a sweet moment and the perfect way to cap my first season with Manchester United.

ABOVE: I thought I was about to double our lead at Wembley when Gordon Banks dived at my feet and I skipped away from him before he could get a finger on the ball. I had fleeting visions of shooting into an empty net, but the Leicester defender on the right, Richie Norman, got back just in time to clear off the line.

GORDON BANKS:

Denis had a fantastic game at Wembley that day. He really lit the place up, and we suffered for his brilliance. That performance set a very high standard, but he more than lived up to it down the years.

OPPOSITE: This was the moment I knew the FA Cup was in the bag. With only five minutes left, Gordon Banks made an uncharacteristic error, dropping a cross from Johnny Giles at the feet of David Herd, who cracked the ball into the net to stretch our lead to 3-1. I was on hand, ready to offer assistance, but my services were not required. After that we could just enjoy the rest of the game, which was not a scenario Leicester could have envisaged because they started as favourites, having finished near the top of the First Division table. We were in the unusual situation of underdogs, yet for perhaps the first time in the whole season we clicked and played as a team. Sadly, the status of the FA Cup is much diminished now. But in those days to score a goal in a Wembley final, and to win, was every footballer's dream – and mine had just come true.

ABOVE: Drama queen? Not me! I'm just reacting to my header against the post from a David Herd cross. The ball beat Gordon Banks, only to bounce back into his arms, and he had the good grace to look both surprised and grateful. This happened after Herdie had put us two up, then Ken Keyworth had pulled one back for Leicester with about ten minutes to go. It could have been a crucial near-miss, but on the other hand, with a bit of luck I could have had a cup final hat-trick. The Leicester defenders – left to right, Ian King, Graham Cross, Richie Norman and Frank McLintock – don't appear quite as emotional as me.

DAVID HERD:

Denis was a top man to have at your side and a fabulous footballer, one of the best there has been. He was brilliant in the FA Cup final to round off his first season with United and I have nothing but happy memories of him.

OPPOSITE: Knackered but ecstatic, David Herd and I head for the Wembley dressing room clutching the spoils of victory. I'm finding out exactly what a winner's medal looks like, while David has the base of the famous old trophy in his custody. Having scored all the goals between us, I suppose we could reflect on a job well done. At that moment, probably I was thinking that I'd scaled the mountain and if I never did it again it wouldn't matter. Big mistake! We should have made it to Wembley on three or four more occasions, but we lost a whole succession of semis. Why? Our squad wasn't big enough to cope with key players carrying long-term injuries, but I don't want to make excuses.

As for playing alongside Herdie, I loved it. He was there when I made my international debut and I always thought of him as a fellow Scot, even though he grew up in Manchester, with the accent to prove it. He was an unselfish runner, brilliant at laying the ball off to me, and he packed a shot that would floor an elephant. Though he contributed 20-odd goals every season like clockwork, he tended to be underrated by some of the fans, but never by the players. We understood his worth, and it was immense.

ABOVE: Swigging Moët in the Wembley dressing room after winning the FA Cup – smashing! Actually, considering how stingy United could be, certainly with our bonuses, I doubt if there was anything in the bottle. In fact, if it wasn't empty I'd say that a photographer had provided it as a prop, just to get the picture.

At this point, I was looking forward to the big banquet that night, then the procession back in Manchester the next day. Watching the winning team arrive home on an open-topped bus, showing the FA Cup to the fans, used to be part and parcel of English life, something special like the Grand National or the Boat Race.

I used to love FA Cup final day, even when I wasn't playing, and it's such a shame that the occasion has lost its lustre. A few of us would meet up at a mate's house around midday, enjoy some bacon and eggs, then out would come the beer while we watched the lead-in on the box. The lubrication would continue throughout the match and we'd be bladdered by teatime. What a wonderful tradition!

But now I hardly ever watch it. It's all become very commercialised and with so many clubs treating the competition lightly it has lost its magic. I find that so, so sad.

ABOVE: You can see by the glazed look in my eyes that I'm nursing a giant hangover, as well as a cigarette – how times change! – as we travel back to Manchester on the morning after the FA Cup final. In fact, our trainer Jack Crompton might even be holding me upright in my seat, so dreadful do I feel. Jack, of course, was as bright as a button. He would have a drink with us, but he always knew when to stop.

Jack was Old Trafford's Mr Steady and a big influence around the club. He was a member of Matt Busby's first great team, the one that won the FA Cup in 1948, which made him part of United's history, and he returned to help out after Munich.

With Jack, everything had to be right, and the club was all that mattered. For instance, he sorted the boots and they had to be completely worn out before you got a new pair. He was very old school and would never sanction what he saw as over-spending.

Jack always spoke very quietly, so that sometimes it was difficult to be sure what he was saying. The conversation here? Depends who was on the other side of the table, but he might have been speculating on whether I'd be dried out in time for the next season.

ABOVE: At first I couldn't figure out why I was jumping for joy, and then it came to me – Crerand had finally bought a round . . .

PADDY CRERAND:

Let me tell you about Denis – he was the tightest of the lot! He got a friend of his, an engineer, to split a couple of pennies and put them back together as a double header and a double tailer. When we went to London we'd toss up to see who'd buy the sweets or whatever, and usually it was David Herd who got caught. But one day Denis tossed his dodgy penny in the air and when it landed it split in two. Unmasked at last!

ABOVE: Paddy Crerand is clearly not impressed as I pull up and wind down my car window for a pressman after a pre-season training session. Paddy was a mate of mine – I knew him pretty well even before he came to United from Celtic – but it's fair to say he could be a wee bit impatient, especially in his younger days.

I'm driving a maroon Jaguar, which I had bought because I had become a family man and needed a bigger car. The guy in the showroom was a massive United man and a friend of Matt Busby so I got an unbelievable deal – £750 on the road. I loved that car and I loved the price, too.

PADDY CRERAND:

That's not impatience on my face, it's sheer relief that he's not roaring off at 100 mph. Denis was a mad driver, absolutely crackers.

ABOVE: It's a bit of an understatement to say I wasn't the most popular person at Villa Park when the referee gave me my marching orders in November 1963. As I was escorted to the tunnel I was subjected to a tirade of jeers and insults, and a few apple cores and bits of rubbish came my way, too. It was the first time I'd ever been sent off and it was for following a maxim I'd grown up with – if somebody kicks you, then you kick 'em back. You have to stand up for yourself or they'll bully you forever.

One of the Villa defenders had been fouling me persistently. I warned him what would happen if he didn't stop, but he took no notice and I didn't have the will to hold back. It was always my problem that the referee would miss the original offence, then home in on my retaliation. I wouldn't be devious enough to wait for a sneaky dig, like some players I could name. Of course, I was disappointed to be dismissed but I didn't beat myself up about it. No way was I going to be kicked, and I knew for sure the next time I played against the same guy he wouldn't be kicking me.

It goes back to my schooldays when the kid across the road used to frighten me to death. He would whack me and I'd run home to avoid him, but then one day I'd had enough and I gave him a hiding. After that, believe it or not, we became the best of pals.

BELOW: When you know you're going to be out for a month, it's nice to sign off with a few goals, and that's exactly what I managed to do when Stoke City were the visitors to Old Trafford in December 1963. We won 5-2, I scored four times, and then headed off to Aberdeen to spend Christmas by the fireside with a bottle of beer in my hand while the rest of the lads were braving the snow and the rain down in England. Lovely. I'm sure Paddy really appreciated that!

I can say categorically that I didn't pull out any more stops because I was on the verge of suspension. I couldn't do that anyway because I always gave my all in every game. It was just that the chances came along and I was lucky enough to put them away.

Here I'm giving a pat on the back to former United player Dennis Viollet, who was a tremendous footballer and a smashing lad, and it was a rare privilege to be involved in a game with the incomparable Stanley Matthews (left), who was nearly 50 at the time. Simply incredible! I can't see anyone ever playing to that age at the top level in the modern game.

ABOVE: Now, this is one hell of a curiosity. Here am I attempting to run through the massed ranks of the Spurs rearguard, and one of the men trying to stop me is the greatest pure goal-scorer I have ever seen. We should treasure this picture because never before do I recall seeing Jimmy Greaves – he's the mud-spattered figure fourth from the left – battling away alongside his defenders. On second thoughts, I don't believe it. Somebody must have tampered with the photograph and put his head on another player's body!

The White Hart Lane pitch was an absolute quagmire that afternoon in March 1964, the sort of surface that would be a real culture shock for the footballers of today. Part of the reason for the squelching swamps of our era was that much of the day-to-day training was done on the pitches, so it was hardly surprising that by mid-winter we were up to our ankles in the brown stuff. Of course, this is where the tough guys came into their own, people like big Maurice Norman on the right. Still, though, the really skilful individuals could perform brilliantly. Goals were scored and the fans were entertained.

The full cast of this mudlark is, left to right, Alan Mullery, Peter Baker, Cliff Jones, Jimmy Greaves, myself (partially obscuring Bobby Charlton) and Maurice Norman.

JIMMY GREAVES:

Denis is absolutely right. Clearly someone has superimposed my head on another body, probably Dave Mackay's, because he would have been battling away somewhere in there. Certainly, I was never impressed with the new-fangled ideas that had forwards running everywhere like blue-assed flies. My job was at the other end of the pitch, and if everyone did their own job it was to the advantage of the team.

As for Denis, he was my favourite footballer – a truly great player and a smashing lad.

ABOVE: I'm waiting for a rebound that never came, but I'm celebrating anyway because Bobby Charlton has just scored at White Hart Lane with one of his trademark long-range howitzers that has left keeper John Hollowbread face down in the mud.

One of the main reasons I loved playing with Bobby and David Herd, who carried an even more powerful shot, was the number of goals I managed to nick through nipping in to tuck away rebounds. As soon as I saw either of them line up to shoot, I would be on my toes ready to pounce. By doing that, often I could distract the keeper and lots of unconsidered trifles came my way. Sadly, I was never in a position to reciprocate – if I hit a shot from outside the box, probably it wouldn't even reach the goal!

This effort of Bobby's went in on that same spring afternoon in 1964 when Greavsie somehow wandered into defence. In the end he needn't have bothered because we won 3-2.

BOBBY CHARLTON:

It was a joy to line up alongside Denis, to know that if I could find a bit of space on either wing then I would be certain to find him with a cross to my near post. And how he would fight for that ball, no matter how physically intimidating the opposing centre-half might be. I have never witnessed a fiercer competitor than Denis Law – and it would be the stuff of nightmares to imagine one!

LEFT: This Old Trafford handshake with Charlie Hurley, the giant Irishman who skippered Sunderland in the 1960s and was arguably the best British centre-half of his generation, signalled the start of an FA Cup marathon of a type now consigned to history. This was the first of three games with the Second Division Wearsiders before the quarter-final was settled, and in all honesty United were lucky to go through. We drew 3-3 at home, with late goals from Bobby and George saving our bacon, then Bobby rescued us again with an extra-time strike in the 2-2 draw at Roker Park before we prevailed 5-1 in the second replay at Huddersfield, where I scored a hat-trick.

We were going for the treble of European Cup-Winners' Cup, League Championship and FA Cup, but we finished with nothing, our cause not helped by having to play seven games in the space of 17 days. That couldn't happen now because multiple FA Cup replays are a thing of the past, which I think is fairer on the fans who have to spend a fortune to travel. That said, nobody likes getting beaten on penalties.

OPPOSITE: I'm looking supremely confident ahead of kick-off against Sporting Lisbon in March 1964, but after 90 minutes of barely believable action that carefree grin was wiped from my face. Let me explain. After the Old Trafford leg of our European Cup-Winners' Cup quarter-final, United were sitting on a 4-1 lead and contemplating the last four. We should have scored more at home, but our profligacy hadn't seemed to matter. The alarm bells were hardly ringing, either, when I hit the post early in the second encounter and another opportunity went begging.

But then the roof fell in. We played like drains, suffered one disaster after another and went down 5-0 on the night to return the most shocking result in the modern history of our club. No professionals should fall apart like that, and in the dressing room afterwards it was entirely appropriate that Matt Busby delivered one of his extremely rare bollockings, telling us we were a disgrace and that our performance was an insult to our fans. We couldn't argue with him because he was absolutely right.

ABOVE: One of the most surreal experiences of my footballing life was wandering on to the set of the epic film *55 Days In Peking* when we were in, er, Spain for a friendly with Real Madrid in the mid-1960s. We met the star, Charlton Heston, and played with some of the props, such as this elephant gun. Who have I got in my sights? It might have been Real's Francisco Gento, but more likely it was Paddy Crerand. It was amazing to stroll among the Oriental towers and minarets that had been recreated in minute detail outside the Spanish capital. The only disappointment was that we didn't catch up with the female lead, Ava Gardner. I guess she must have seen us coming and stayed in her caravan.

ABOVE: I reckon I deserved a pay-off here from Edward Wood of Manchester and London for advertising their steelworks, but I'm still waiting! More to the point, despite the fact that my eyes are glued to the ball, I'm slightly misconnecting with a cross from Graham Moore, who was performing very impressively on his debut for United against Spurs at Old Trafford in November 1963.

We played really well as a team that day. I managed a hat-trick and we won 4-1, but we had enough chances to have piled up a few more goals. Goalkeeper Bill Brown, my Scotland team-mate, is looking uncharacteristically flat-footed and I reckon I might have beaten him if my header had been on target. The other Spurs man pictured is another Scottish pal, John White. Tragically he had only a few more months to live.

BELOW: 'Glad you're cleaning yourself up. I'm just off to take the Queen for a drink, and I can hardly go to the bar with muddy hands.' That *might* have been what the Duke of Edinburgh said to me as he prepared to hand me the trophy after United beat City in a friendly game for a children's charity at Maine Road in May 1964. On the other hand, maybe it wasn't.

We'd had a brilliantly enjoyable game in the pelting rain, I'd scored a hat-trick and it was lovely to see smiles on the faces of everybody, including United chairman Louis Edwards (centre). The Duke was pretty chipper, ready to join in a joke with a collection of saturated footballers who had just crawled off a paddyfield, and I found that very refreshing.

You see people coming away from games today and you'd think they'd lost family. Excuse me! Football is a game and it needs a sense of proportion. Nobody wanted my team to win more than me, but really, it's not the end of the world if you lose. I always agreed with Matt Busby that, as long as you've tried your best, the result makes no difference. That attitude used to be widespread, but with the advent of so much money in the game the result has become everything, which makes everything so grim.

On a lighter tack, hasn't the Duke worn well? He doesn't look much different today than he did on that filthy night in Manchester nearly half a century ago.

CHAPTER 7

IN THE COMPANY OF LEGENDS

ABOVE: When the news came through that England were to play the Rest of the World at Wembley to celebrate the Football Association's centenary in the autumn of 1963, at first the information went in one ear and out the other. But when I discovered that I was picked for the team to play England, and that I would be lining up alongside some of the finest footballers who ever lived, including my all-time hero Alfredo di Stefano, it was an absolutely unimaginable honour.

Even looking at this picture now, nearly half a century later, I can scarcely credit the sight of the great Alfredo in the middle of the front row with his arm draped across *my* shoulder.

If you asked me to name the proudest moment of my career, I'd have to say that it was being asked to play for my country, but selection to represent the Rest of the World comes not too far adrift. We were even playing in blue shirts, though the shade was a tad lighter than I was used to.

Facing the camera on the lush Wembley turf are, back row left to right: Ferenc Puskas, Djalma Santos, Svatopluk Pluskal, Lev Yashin, Jan Popluhar, Karl-Heinz Schnellinger, Milutin Soskic, Josef Masopust, Luis Eyzaguirre, Uwe Seeler. Front row: Raymond Kopa, myself, Alfredo di Stefano, Eusebio, Francisco Gento. Unfortunately my Scottish pal Jim Baxter, who also played, is obscured behind Eyzaguirre.

ABOVE: I was lucky enough to be selected for two representative matches that transcended national boundaries. First came the Rest of the World game against England in October 1963, and then at the end of that season I was called up for the Rest of Europe, who faced Scandinavia in Copenhagen to mark the 75th anniversary of the Danish FA. For a young lad from Printfield Terrace, this was heaping privilege upon privilege.

ABOVE: It was as if I had died and gone to heaven. There I was running around on the smooth green acres of Wembley, exchanging passes with the likes of Alfredo di Stefano, Ferenc Puskas and Eusebio. I might have owed my presence in the Rest of the World starting line-up to the fact that Pelé was injured, but if that was the case, it certainly didn't lessen my enjoyment of the occasion. I was fortunate enough to play for the whole 90 minutes and I was delighted to be joined for the second half by Jim Baxter. I'll remember that day as long as I live.

Law and disorder . . . !

Denis Law bites the dust in a not very immaculate manner while playing for the Rest of Europe against Scandinavia.

ABOVE: This looks like I'm wishing the ground would open and swallow me up, and maybe goalkeeper Sverre Andersen reckons that's not the worst idea I've ever had. I've just flown through the air at full throttle in a vain attempt to score for the Rest of Europe against Scandinavia and I've fallen just short, you might call it comically short, of the goal-line. Certainly Andersen, the venerable Norwegian net-minder, sees the funny side of it. Well, if he wants to be a comedian, all I can say is that he's got a bigger nose than me – maybe not the cleverest of punchlines, but the best I can manage in the circumstances.

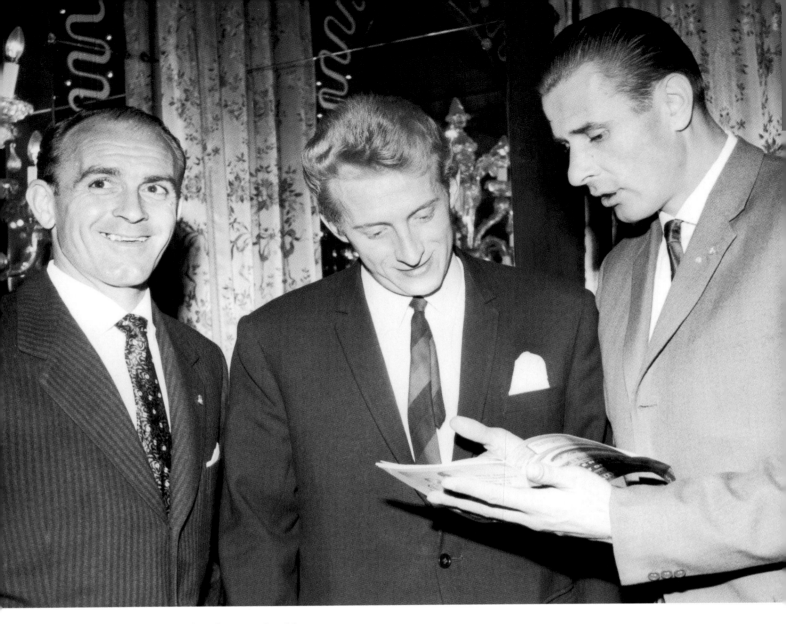

ABOVE: There is an old saying that you should never meet your heroes, but whoever came up with that notion had obviously never encountered Alfredo di Stefano. Not only was he the sublime performer on the pitch that I had always believed him to be, but he was a lovely, everyday kind of guy, too. Here Alfredo (left) and I are looking at the match programme with Lev Yashin, the magnificent Russian goalkeeper, who turned out to be another smashing bloke. We weren't all together for very long, but we had a tremendous time at our London hotel, and I'll never forget Jim Baxter extolling the virtues of Scotch whisky to the likes of Alfredo and Ferenc Puskas. I have to say they caught on pretty quickly!

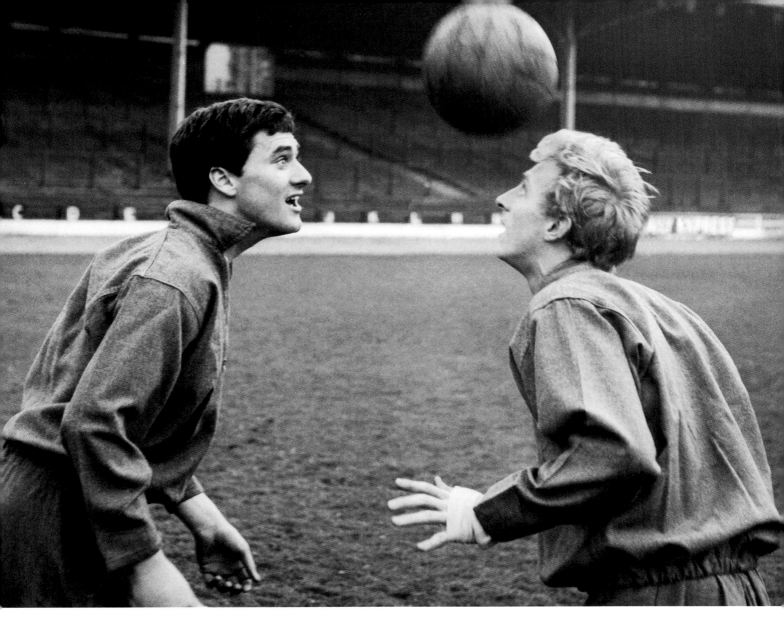

ABOVE: Heading practice with my pal Jim Baxter, the only other Brit in the Rest of the World squad. When it came to training, Jim loathed running round the track as much as he loved playing with the ball. He used to have endless arguments with our Scotland trainers over what their priorities should be.

In games he could be a bit frustrating at times, because he would hang on to the ball for so long. You would sprint into position and often it wouldn't come to you. Just as with Bestie on occasions, you'd give him an earful, but then, likely as not, he would shut you up by scoring a sensational goal. Jim was a sublime passer who took your breath away with his accuracy and imagination, and he was the creative brains of any team he was in. The beauty of playing with great footballers is that they make the game simple for their team-mates. They always seem to have time and space, which means there is always an out ball for us mere mortals to pass to.

As for Jim's personality, he was just Jack the lad, full of mischief the whole time. Might he have been an ideal signing for United? Well, by the time he was available, Matt Busby had already recruited Paddy Crerand, another forthright individual and brilliantly constructive operator, so the blend wouldn't have been right. Might have been interesting, though ...

ABOVE: This is the goal that crowned my experience of playing for the Rest of the World, even though we lost 2-1 to England. Ferenc Puskas picked up the ball in the inside-left position some 40 yards from goal and strode forward. I was darting down the inside-right channel, thinking I might cause a diversion to allow the incomparable 'Galloping Major' to employ his prodigious left-foot shot. But I shouted his name and to my astonishment he arrowed this perfect pass to my feet, enabling me to run on and beat Gordon Banks with a low side-foot. Gordon is a pal of mine, but it was no problem, sorry mate!

Many of the Rest of the World players didn't speak much English, but football is a universal language and they just let it flow. If they'd had more time together they'd have been even better but, trust me, for a one-off their performance wasn't too shabby. Although it was essentially an exhibition match, it was played at a proper tempo; at least that's how I treated it. After all, why would I want to go easy on England at Wembley?

ABOVE: This was one of the most satisfying games I ever played in. The date was 6 April 1963, the venue was Wembley and we beat England 2-1, thanks to a couple of goals from the elegant 'Slim Jim' Baxter. Why so special? Well, it was Scotland's first victory on English soil for a dozen years and it went some way towards making up for our previous appearance at the famous old stadium, when they tell me we went down 9-3. I think that'll do for a start! What made Scotland's display even more praiseworthy was that we played with ten men for 85 minutes after our skipper Eric Caldow suffered a fractured leg in a challenge with England centre-forward Bobby Smith.

Here a cross has come in and Ian St John (right) has launched himself at it in typical committed fashion, but Gordon Banks, making his full international debut, has managed to cut it out. Bobby Moore is protecting his keeper and I'm lurking in the hope of a fumble, which didn't happen very often with Gordon.

OPPOSITE: A vigorous coming together with England's Jimmy Armfield, who has just thwarted my attempt to get on the Wembley scoresheet. He was a real gentleman, but he could get stuck in when necessary, as he demonstrates here. Yet earlier in the game he had made an uncharacteristic error, being caught in possession by Jim Baxter, who scored the first of his two goals. Mind, Baxter was in his pomp then, enjoying the sort of day when he could have walked on water without getting his feet wet.

Jimmy Armfield was a superbly classy right-back and loyal, too, spending the whole of his illustrious career with Blackpool, which ended sadly when the Seasiders were relegated from the top flight at the end of his final match in 1971. At this point he was also England captain, and nobody could have forecast that he would lose his place to the younger George Cohen ahead of the World Cup triumph of 1966.

ABOVE: Look at that scoreboard behind the dear old *Radio Times* logo – it reads England 0, Scotland 2. Aaaah, it did the heart good! In this attack I'm chasing a third goal, hoping to nip past centre-half Maurice Norman, but it looks as if he's got a toe to the ball and nicked it away. Maurice was a very tough customer who played in the heart of defence for Bill Nicholson's great Spurs combination that in 1961 became the first team in the 20th century to win the League and FA Cup double. There have not been many English sides to compare with them in my lifetime.

CHAPTER 8

CHAMPIONS AGAIN

ABOVE: With the familiar old factory chimneys in Trafford Park still towering over the ground, the Manchester United squad face the cameras ahead of the 1964-65 campaign, which was to climax with our first league title since the calamity at Munich. This was my third season at the club, and since my arrival there had been two hugely significant additions to our attacking options. A certain young man from Belfast had risen through the youth ranks and England winger John Connelly had been purchased from Burnley.

There's plenty about George Best elsewhere between these covers, so here I will concentrate on John, who might not have looked like a footballer at first glance – he was more like some immaculate businessman, with his hair always tidy and his boots always shining – but who was actually a top performer. John didn't mess about. He'd tear down the touchline, beat his defender and then, bonk, the ball would be in the box. His service was made for the likes of David Herd and me, but his contribution didn't end there. John was also a major goalscorer in his own right, knocking in 20 during 1964-65, and he worked back to help the defence, as well, not being afraid to put his foot in where it hurts.

He was a grand lad, too, and his presence increased our belief that we were ready to become champions again.

Back row, left to right: Matt Busby, Noel Cantwell, David Sadler, Bill Foulkes, Shay Brennan, David Herd, Harry Gregg, David Gaskell, Graham Moore, Maurice Setters, Paddy Crerand, assistant manager Jimmy Murphy. Front row: Bobby Charlton, Ian Moir, Albert Quixall, John Connelly, Nobby Stiles, George Best, Tony Dunne and myself.

JOHN CONNELLY:

It was a wonderful set-up at Old Trafford with fantastic team spirit, and a lot of that was down to Denis. Usually he had a big grin on his face and he kept everybody bubbling. The only time you didn't want to see Denis was if you were playing for England against Scotland. Then it wasn't a bad idea to keep out of his way.

I counted myself so lucky to play alongside people like Denis, Bobby and George. I could put in a bad cross and they were that brilliant they could make it look like I'd delivered a great ball.

One thing I'll never forget about Denis was the way he pulled his sleeves down over his hands. For a long time after I arrived in Manchester I thought his hands must be deformed!

ABOVE: I know I've just been made the European Footballer of the Year for 1964 because I'm cradling the trophy in my hands, but I don't think full realisation of the scale of the honour sank in until after I had retired. On the day, Matt Busby and my team-mates all said 'well done', but there wasn't a huge amount of attention in the media – that's how it used to be. Now everyone goes mad, the actual trophy is physically bigger and the surrounding fuss seems to go on forever.

On mature reflection, certainly, the award was the pinnacle of my career. After all, the first winner was the incomparable Stanley Matthews in 1956 and I was only the second Brit to be chosen. I think it helped that I had played for the Rest of the World, and that I'd had a spell in Italy, thus making my name familiar to the European journalists who decide the destination of the Ballon D'Or. When I consider some of the fabulous people who have won it – the likes of di Stefano, Eusebio, Suarez and Sivori, and of course Bobby and George a little later – it does make me feel both humble and proud. I'm still the only Scot to have won it and, unfortunately, I can't see that changing in the near future.

OPPOSITE: Somebody must have told me the race was over and my horse was still running! Actually, I'd just been guilty of a terrible miss and I was feeling bad about it, just like the fans. Or had I dropped a spectacular clanger at the back? No, it's stretching credibility just too far to suggest I was helping out our defence.

I guess maybe expressing my emotion on the field in this way was part of the reason why so many Manchester United supporters seemed to identify with me. I would stress, though, that it was all completely spontaneous. I never produced any premeditated reaction to an incident, as I feel some players do today. It was simply that, as might happen to anybody, I was guilty of a cock-up at work and I wasn't happy about it.

ABOVE: I'm not looking too good here, lying sprawled among the boots, and it's hardly surprising because I've just clashed heads with Sunderland centre-half Charlie Hurley in a combative encounter with the newly promoted Wearsiders at Old Trafford in October 1964. Eventually, they dragged me off the field for a few minutes until I stopped seeing two of everything, though I managed to return to help claim a 1-0 win, thanks to a late goal from David Herd. As for Charlie, he wouldn't have felt it anyway – he was made of granite.

Because of the way I played I did spend a fair portion of my time in horizontal mode. Everybody who played up front had to take the knocks and I wasn't as big as some of them, the likes of Spurs' Bobby Smith and Derek Kevan of West Bromwich Albion and Manchester City. It wasn't the most pleasant aspect of the game, but it was unavoidable.

PADDY CRERAND:

I didn't score many so I remember them all. This was a nice little chip over the keeper's head, and to do that at Anfield was fabulous. Denis might be right that it was the fastest I ever moved. Bill Shankly used to say that I was slower than I looked – but I wasn't slow that day!

OPPOSITE: This is one of the best football photographs I've ever seen – not because I'm in it, but because it's a wonderful piece of work. What strikes me first is all the young faces in the crowd. That dates it for a start, because it must have been when kids could afford tickets to watch a top-flight game, a huge contrast with today.

Looking at my upside down self, I love the way my eyes are fixed on the ball. It's a study in complete concentration. Obviously, though, I've realised there's a painful impact in the offing as I've got my hand out to break my fall, which might go some way towards explaining why I have had so much trouble with my wrist and my back later in life.

I guess these acrobatics must have come naturally to me, but looking at it now I can hardly credit that I could have been so foolhardy. Certainly I wasn't daft enough to try it in training, only in the heat of battle, but even that was pretty crazy. After all, I bet the high-jumper Dick Fosbury, creator of the Fosbury Flop, wouldn't have thrown himself around without plenty of foam rubber to land on.

The ball looks as though it's creeping under the crossbar, though I can't be sure if I scored here. The photographer definitely did, though – it's an exceptional picture.

ABOVE: Celebrating a goal at Anfield on a misty Saturday afternoon in the autumn of 1964 – aaah, life can be so, so sweet. Actually, this is something of an oddity, for one compelling reason. The scorer is the fellow dancing a jig in the No 4 shirt and it's Paddy Crerand. It looks like that might be the fastest he ever moved in his life. Certainly it's the only time I've ever seen him with two feet off the ground. After David Herd had put us in front in the first half, Paddy's effort on the hour virtually sealed the points, and the two Liverpool men on the right, wing-half Gordon Milne and goalkeeper Tommy Lawrence, know that only too well.

To record a 2-0 victory at Liverpool, especially when they were the reigning champions, was a crucial step towards capturing their crown. During this era, whoever came out on top in United–Liverpool confrontations usually went on to win the League.

Afterwards I had a chat with my old boss Bill Shankly, who was a big pal of Matt Busby and was a familiar sight at Old Trafford. Often he would turn up if his own club didn't have a game. He wouldn't have taken this defeat very well, his verdict being along the lines of 'We were robbed'. According to Shanks, the ref would have been garbage, his team would have missed four open goals and United would have been lucky, no matter how the game had gone in reality.

OPPOSITE: From this distance, the sight of a goalkeeper diving on the ball with his head in close proximity to my flailing feet makes me cringe. It's so easy to kick a keeper accidentally and the consequences can be frightening. Some of them, like Fulham's Tony Macedo here, were so incredibly brave. They had only to mishandle the ball slightly to set up a 50:50 situation with the attacker, and they knew that sooner or later they were going to be hurt. I guess that's why keepers have to be a bit bonkers in the first place.

Often, of course, the forward came off worse. Keepers are almost always big lads and many's the time they come flying at you four feet off the ground with their elbows and knees sticking out all over the place. They know how to protect themselves, all right. That said, there's no way I would have played in goal myself . . .

ABOVE: Sometimes the work of a front-man has to be done in the blink of an eye. There's no stopping to ponder what might be best, just instant reflex reaction. That's the Chelsea hard man Ronnie Harris's leg on the left. I've got to get my shot in before he comes at me like a bull and batters me. Instinct is all-important. When I'm asked how I did this or that on the field, in all honesty I haven't got a clue. It all happened on the spur of the moment. Watching my effort to score against the Londoners at Old Trafford are team-mates John Connelly (left) and David Herd.

ABOVE: My precise words escape me now, which is just as well, but I know I turned the air blue at Blackpool in November 1964 and was sent off as a result. But even though I swore, no doubt luridly, I was the victim of a gross injustice.

I had been tightly marked by Alan Ball (second left), a fantastic player but also a fiery little so-and-so. There had been a few niggly moments between us and eventually I was booked for fouling him, which is when my problems really started. As the referee, Peter Rhodes, was jotting down my particulars, Paddy Crerand (third from right) wandered over to tell me to calm down. I wasn't too happy with life at that precise moment, so I gave Paddy a mouthful. Trouble was, the ref thought I was talking to him and dismissed me on the spot. Here it looks like Paddy is pleading for me, or maybe he's saying I should have been off half an hour ago!

There was an FA crackdown at the time and I had a feeling they would make an example of me. So it proved. Even though Paddy spoke for me at the hearing, I was suspended for 28 days and fined £50. At the time I felt I was being victimised, and I haven't changed my mind.

ALAN BALL:

I provoked the incident with the great Denis Law that saw us both sent off ... he was blazing mad with me. I felt shocking but I couldn't say anything then. We were together at a dinner in Aberdeen in 2003 and he was on his feet, eyebrows raised, pointing his finger at me and wagging it, saying: 'He's there. Sent off at Blackpool. Cheeky little bastard.'

ABOVE: To say I was resentful over my suspension following the Blackpool incident is selling my feelings a trifle short. Four weeks out of the team without any wages? It was utterly disgraceful, like some horror story from the Middle Ages, and I was seething.

Imagine my sense of release, then, when I returned to action, against Nottingham Forest at the City Ground in January, and scored a couple of goals. I felt like a prisoner who had escaped from jail and it's fair to say there's an extra edge to this celebration, although beaten goalkeeper Peter Grummitt looks understandably unimpressed. The match finished 2-2, with Alan Hinton scoring both their goals.

ABOVE: Going by the fur hat, which reminds me of Bobby Charlton's preferred winter headgear these days, I might be confronting Lev Yashin . . . or is it Leonid Brezhnev? Actually it's a moment of light relief on a tense Easter Monday at St Andrews, Birmingham, on the run-in to United's first League Championship since Munich.

My failed effort to beat City goalkeeper Johnny Schofield had left me flat out on the by-line, face to face with a friendly photographer, who was ideally kitted out for a bracing afternoon on which I recall there were snow flurries.

The game was a roller coaster, with bottom-placed Birmingham desperate for points to avoid relegation. We led 1-0, then went 2-1 behind, before winning 4-2 thanks to a spell of three goals in 12 second-half minutes. The day finished with us climbing above Leeds and Chelsea to top the table, while Birmingham's demotion was confirmed.

OPPOSITE: There weren't many rival captains that I towered over, but Bobby Collins of Leeds United was one of them. He was a fiery little competitor who certainly taught Johnny Giles a thing or two after the Irishman moved to Elland Road from Old Trafford. Bobby was a clever and combative inside-forward who always punched more than his weight on the pitch, but was a lovely friendly guy off it. When I won my first cap, he was a household name and I was a nobody, but he went out of his way to look after me and make me feel at home.

This handshake was ahead of our semi-final at Hillsborough on a pitch which had been smoothed over like the top of a chocolate cake, but which in reality was a cloying mess. The exchanges were good-natured at this stage but then, as we shall see, battle was joined with a vengeance, as might be expected from two teams who were neck-and-neck for the League and FA Cup double.

ABOVE: Perhaps the FA were trying to make me feel at home, for once, when they booked a band of girl pipers to greet the Uniteds of Manchester and Leeds as we walked out at Hillsborough in March 1965 for our FA Cup semi-final – but I doubt it.

I was always proud to lead out my team, whether at schoolboy, club or international level, but I never saw myself as one fellow in charge of the rest. Every good team needs a few captains, motivators who will keep the lads going at all times. We were lucky, having the likes of Paddy Crerand and Nobby Stiles, who were shouting directions to the rest of us the whole time.

Following me out here are Pat Dunne, David Herd and George Best, while I'm certain I've spotted another familiar face in the crowd. Just to the left of my head as you look at the picture is Gordon Banks, who must have been keen to watch the game but couldn't persuade the FA to find him a place in the directors' box. Either that, or Gordon's got a twin he's never told us about.

ABOVE: It's fair to say that tempers became a wee bit frayed in our FA Cup semi-final encounter with Leeds on a Hillsborough mudheap, but despite this photographic evidence, for me newspaper descriptions of a brawl rather over-egged the violence. I saw no blood and heard precious little thunder. True, during one frank exchange of views, Jack Charlton did practically rip my shirt from my back, but then it's just possible that I might have provoked him somewhere along the line. Maybe I accused him of not buying his round!

Clearly his brother Bobby is experiencing some strife while attempting to act as a peacemaker between Paddy Crerand and Billy Bremner, two of my countrymen renowned for their, er, forthright approach. Meanwhile, Bobby Collins appears to be tugging me away from Jack, while George Best opts to stay out of the mêlée, even though it wouldn't surprise me if he was the cause of it.

Whatever else, this is a great picture. See that crowd, transfixed by the unscheduled action, with Jack looking as though he had a gun in his hand. At that point, probably he wished he had.

OPPOSITE: In this shot, in which my shirt is still intact, I must admit it looks as though I'm contemplating fisticuffs with the big fella, but I don't believe I ever threw the punch. This was just a negotiating position! Certainly, I wasn't sent off and neither was anybody else. I was a friend of Jack and there were no grudges. I'm pretty sure we had a drink together after the game, which finished goalless, then we lost the replay 1-0.

JACK CHARLTON:

Denis was always a pal of mine and I still think the world of him today. I've got two or three of his shirts at home that I ripped off his back. I think he must have been running away from me at the time!

He was a great competitor, so sharp, tremendous in the air. There was one time at Elland Road when he dived over me to reach a cross, heading the ball into the net. Totally accidentally, I kicked him in the mouth when I was following through, and it didn't look good as he lay still on the ground with blood everywhere. But then as he started to come round, he looked up at me and smiled, and I'll never forget his words: 'Did I score, big fella?'

RIGHT: This shot might be used in evidence against me when I mount one of my many hobbyhorses, specifically the one condemning excessive celebration of goals in the modern game. Here I'm saluting the travelling United fans after scoring only four minutes into our meeting with Everton at Goodison Park in September 1964. In fact, I think I can be excused my fleeting expression of glee on a wet Merseyside night, and it doesn't alter my contention that nowadays many of the reactions to finding the net are somewhat over the top.

I find it difficult to see why players have to rip off their shirt, or unveil a T-shirt with a message, or perform some minutely rehearsed dance. Like as not they'll be kissing their badge one week, then the next demand to leave the club because they want more money. At the risk of sounding grumpy (who, me?) I wish they would keep a little perspective.

Maybe I should have followed my own advice here, because by the end of the evening United had squandered a two-goal lead, having to settle for a 3-3 draw. Bah, humbug!

OPPOSITE: Sometimes being a footballer can really hurt. I had just scored a goal that put United two up against Liverpool early in the second half at Old Trafford in the spring of 1965. Now the title was virtually ours for the taking, so I must have felt that the pain was worth it – right? Wrong! I was in agony and all that occupied my mind in that instant was that I wanted it to stop.

My caring team-mate Paddy Crerand is doing his best to comfort me with the cold sponge, and telling me not to look as trainer Jack Crompton examines the gash on my knee which followed a collision with the net stanchion during my celebration of beating Liverpool goalkeeper Tommy Lawrence (left). Behind me George Best, who knows what it's like to take physical punishment himself, offers some well-meant words of sympathy which barely register.

Having scored both our goals, I went off to receive six stitches in the wound and returned to the action near the end, only as a passenger. I wasn't really needed anyway, as John Connelly added a third to complete a crucial victory. Meanwhile, Matt Busby was already telling me that I *would* be fit to face Arsenal two nights later . . .

ABOVE: I can shoot down a myth here. Even though I had ripped my knee horribly against Liverpool, it was reported widely that I'd have to be restrained physically to prevent me from taking the field against Arsenal at Old Trafford only some 48 hours later, in the game which could virtually confirm Manchester United as league champions for 1964-65.

Excuse me! I had just had six stitches in the joint, which was extremely tender, and I thought there was absolutely no way I should be playing. But Matt Busby would have none of it and told me I'd be in the team. When I gaped and pointed at my knee, he just said: 'Ah, you'll be all right. Just get out there and play.' So what choice did I have? The wound was

sprayed to deaden the pain and covered with a plaster, then trainer Jack Crompton freshened me up with his dreaded cold sponge before sending me out to do battle with the Gunners.

Of course, once I was on the pitch I never thought any more about the injury. There was no point, I just had to get on with it. As it turned out, the manager could claim vindication. George Best put us in front early on, I added another on the hour, then George Eastham pulled one back for Arsenal before I knocked in this clincher after David Herd had hit the bar. Afterwards Matt just smiled and said: 'Well done, son. I knew you'd be all right.'

ABOVE: We had not been mathematically confirmed as champions by beating Arsenal, but as it would have taken a 19-0 defeat in our final game at Villa Park to deprive us of the crown, it didn't seem excessively naughty to pop the champagne corks in the Old Trafford dressing room after overcoming the north Londoners. By this time my knee was smarting again, but somehow I mustered the strength to hold out my glass for Matt Busby to pour that longed-for bubbly.

The Boss didn't make any fancy speeches, but his thoughts must have turned to the lads who had won him his previous title, eight years earlier, before the accident at Munich. Also, having been Britain's trailblazer into European competition, he would have been relishing another chance to tilt at the top prize, which had become his equivalent of the Holy Grail.

Joining in the celebrations are, at the back, Shay Brennan (left) and John Connelly, who evidently preferred a beer. Paddy Crerand has his arms around Matt Busby and Pat Dunne, while David Herd is on the right.

OPPOSITE: Don't drop me, boys, I've got a dodgy knee. It was my privileged job as skipper to show the League Championship trophy to the ecstatic Old Trafford faithful before our Inter-Cities Fairs Cup quarter-final first leg encounter with Strasbourg in May 1965. Of the two men keeping me aloft, David Herd (left) seems to be struggling a bit while big Bill Foulkes, the tough-as-teak former coal miner who shored up the centre of our defence, looks as though he could carry me on his own for as long as was required. To round off a perfect day, I managed to tuck away a couple of headers as we beat our French visitors 5-0.

BILL FOULKES:
Drop Denis Law at Old Trafford? It would have been more than my life was worth!

CHAPTER 9

THE BEST YET

ABOVE AND OPPOSITE: If you didn't know that I'd spent a lot of time in Italy, these pictures would furnish a major clue. Nobody will be surprised to learn that I didn't pick up my penchant for extravagant gestures in Aberdeen or Huddersfield or even Manchester. But during my year-long interlude in Turin, aaaah, now that was something else.

As a young lad learning his trade in the solid, unpretentious surroundings of Leeds Road and Maine Road, I would have been clipped round the ear, or even worse, if I had greeted a refereeing decision with the type of flamboyant reaction you

see here. But it's different with Italians. If you cut off their hands they couldn't speak! I was young and impressionable, so it was inevitable that I picked up on the arm-waving.

This demonstrative sequence was captured at Highbury in September 1965, when clearly it left the Arsenal defenders Terry Neill (No 5), Don Howe (No 2) and David Court emphatically underwhelmed. I don't think I made much impression on the referee, either, because we lost 4-2 and I failed to get on the scoresheet. *Così è la vita!*

ABOVE: Understandably enough, the first leg of our 1966 European Cup quarter-final encounter with Benfica at Old Trafford tends to receive little attention in the history books, due to our epic performance in the second leg, in which the mighty Eagles were annihilated 5-1.

Yet there was a fine game at Old Trafford, too, in which we triumphed 3-2. Admittedly we feared that we had not built a big enough lead to take with us to one of the great fortresses of European football. Here the two captains are in direct opposition, with Mario Coluna attempting to block my left-foot shot. He was a classy, clever footballer with a beautiful first touch, and he reminded me very much of the cultured Spurs skipper Danny Blanchflower, a man who could run any game.

Like Danny, too, Mario was a gentleman. Back in the 1960s we used to have banquets after European matches, which gave us a chance to forge personal relationships, a pleasure not afforded to the players of today.

OPPOSITE: Before the serious business started in what was to prove an unforgettable visit to the Stadium of Light, I had a happy duty to perform. As the previous European Footballer of the Year I presented the Ballon D'Or to its new holder, Eusebio of Benfica, a delightfully quiet and modest man, but one of the most explosive talents the game has ever known. I first became friendly with him when we both played for the Rest of the World against England in 1963 and it was a pleasure to renew our acquaintance at such a significant ceremony.

I don't bump into him all that often these days, though when I did see him at a charity do in Portugal I thought he had turned into a dead ringer for Robert Mugabe. Eusebio is a rather more appealing character, and he chuckled at the thought of resembling Zimbabwe's President.

Back in Lisbon in 1966, United turned on the style to win 5-1 and gave what I firmly believe to be that team's finest ever display. It was just one of those magical nights when everything slipped into place. As usual in away games on the continent, the manager had told us to play it tight for 20 minutes, then see where Benfica's weaknesses were before attacking them. But George Best wasn't listening. He just went out and played as only he could, scoring two early goals and setting us up for a sensational overall performance.

It was especially satisfying as we were returning to the city where we had shipped five goals in 1964. Before the game, the Portuguese fans were holding up five fingers in a cheeky prediction. They were proved right, but hardly in the manner they expected.

LEFT: Perhaps unfairly, perhaps not, footballers are not renowned for embracing local culture on their travels around the world, but when Manchester United journeyed to Lisbon to face Benfica early in the spring of 1966 there was a remarkable exception. After the game, the United lads decided to investigate the city and we posed in front of this magnificent memorial to the great Portuguese navigators and explorers who opened up new lands and seaways all over the globe. It was an apt choice, in view of our club's own pioneering exploits, blazing the British trail into Europe during the previous decade.

Left to right, looking exceedingly smart, are John Connelly, Bobby Charlton, Harry Gregg, Paddy Crerand, Matt Busby, George Best, David Herd, Nobby Stiles, myself, Tony Dunne, Shay Brennan and Bill Foulkes, coolest of the lot in his shades. The manager is looking quietly proud of what many have described as his third great team, and he had reason to be, as we had just become the first foreign side to beat Benfica at the Stadium of Light. In truth, we didn't just defeat them, we absolutely murdered them.

ABOVE: Not quite Carrington, is it? Bobby Charlton, Shay Brennan (back to camera) and I take a desperately needed break in a pre-season training session under the south stand at Old Trafford. Compared to United's magnificent modern facilities, ours were pretty primitive and so were some of the methods. For example, we had these ridiculous weights that we could only pretend to lift because they were way too heavy. After all, we were footballers, not candidates to become Mr Universe.

Pre-season was murder, a truly horrible time, but there was no escaping it. Some enjoyed it more than others – Bobby, for instance, didn't mind the running, while I loathed it, as did Bestie. I noticed a huge difference between the English approach and the Italian way, which always involved the ball. They were way ahead of us in that respect.

What am I saying here? 'What a load of rubbish this is – I want to go home!'

LEFT: 'Put it there, Boss. I think we understand each other perfectly.' This was the moment the world was told that I had been taken off the transfer list in July 1966, after apologising for asking for a pay rise. How much extra did I want? A tenner a week! If a Premier League footballer of today found one of those in his pocket, probably he'd use it to light his cigar. It seemed as though I was backing down, but in private I was given my tenner and this was merely an exercise in saving Matt Busby's face. In the end we were both happy – I didn't want to go and he didn't want to sell me.

The manager was invariably portrayed as an avuncular figure, and so he was, but there is no doubt there was an iron fist in that velvet glove. You couldn't run a massive club like Manchester United for a quarter of a century without having a core of steel. He wouldn't give you a bollocking in front of everybody, but he would leave you in no doubt who was in charge. There was a referees' room in the dressing-room corridor and if you had done something wrong the chances were that as you walked past that door on your way to training you would hear a hiss. Matt would be sitting there waiting for you, and he would tell you calmly, but with total authority, exactly what was expected of you in future. He was a father figure and he had our respect because we knew he was scrupulously fair. But he had our affection, too. Every time we ran out to play in front of 60,000, of course we wanted to win for ourselves – but most of all we wanted to win for Matt Busby.

BOBBY CHARLTON:

We're completely knackered. I detested pre-season because it came so hard after the summer holiday, but also because there was no end product in the form of a game. Typically, though, Denis is delivering a quip – I don't know where he got the breath!

OPPOSITE: The clock on the Old Trafford scoreboard signals 16 minutes past three as I rise above West Bromwich Albion's Bobby Cram to put us 3-1 up on the opening day of the 1966-67 campaign. It was an amazing afternoon, with United winning 5-3 after scoring all our goals in the first 22 minutes.

I owed much of the fact that I could climb tolerably well to Bill Shankly during my time at Huddersfield. He'd have a ball strung up underneath the main stand for us to run at and head. Each time you made contact it would be moved a little higher and in this way your spring improved dramatically. It was great fun, too, as he would have 15 guys all trying to outdo each other. Shanks thrived on the competition, and so did his players.

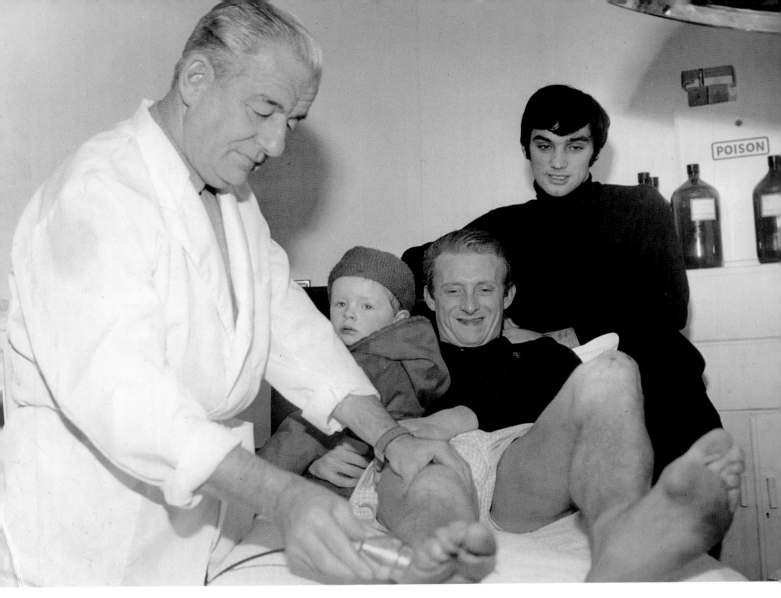

ABOVE: An all too familiar experience for me, sitting on the treatment table being poked and prodded by our physiotherapist 'Uncle Ted' Dalton. At least I'm smiling – or is that a grimace? – while George Best and my son, Gary, are looking decidedly sombre. Perhaps they felt a tad intimidated by the large bottles of poison on the shelf – obviously Uncle Ted was well stocked up in case any of his patients had to be put down!

My legs took a fair old beating and, as I wince at the old war wounds even to this day, I can hardly believe that I never wore shinpads as a professional. I felt restricted in pads, which deadened my touch and reduced my freedom of movement, and I hadn't bothered with them since my schooldays. Mind, in those days we called them paperbacks! In the circumstances I guess I was lucky I never suffered a broken leg, given some of the tough customers around the First Division at the time.

People used to joke that horses got better treatment than injured footballers, who were invariably pumped full of cortisone, the miracle painkiller of the time. The trouble was that players paid the price in later years of managers getting us on the pitch when we were nowhere near fully fit. That was the norm at all clubs, but it was a woefully short-sighted policy. Often by resting for a couple of games you could avoid a six-week lay-off, but nobody seemed to think that far ahead.

LEFT: I've chosen this picture for two reasons. Firstly, because it gives me a chance to talk about Irish international full-back Tony Dunne, one of the most underrated of players and a good pal, and secondly because the caption in the newspaper files was memorably daft. It read: 'Manchester United footballers Denis Law and Tony Dunne practise their goal celebration.' As if! Far more likely, I'm volunteering Tony for crossing practice . . .

Although he wasn't as accurate a passer as Ray Wilson, in all other ways he was similar to England's World Cup-winning left-back. Not many wingers got past Tony, and if they did he was quick enough to get back and make a second challenge. He was brilliant, too, at covering our central defenders, Bill Foulkes and Nobby Stiles, though if he went down the wing with the ball, I knew there was little likelihood of me getting it. You see, I wasn't allowed to fetch it from the Stretford End. The ball had to be on the pitch and, without being unkind, crossing wasn't Tony's strength. He was a get-it-and-give-it-simply type of defender, and as such he had few equals.

Also he was so exceptionally consistent that I can't ever recall him having a bad game, and probably he's the only United player of my generation I could describe in that way. Most important of all, Tony's a lovely lad and the Old Trafford scene would have been much poorer without him.

TONY DUNNE:

Denis didn't need me for his celebrations. He was enough of a showman to do that job himself. As for my crossing, Matt Busby used to give me a rollicking if I went over the halfway line, so I didn't get much practice. He used to say to me: 'Now who do you think I want crossing the ball – Tony Dunne or George Best?' Enough said. These days, Denis has a statue on the Stretford End and all I can say is that he should have been there when we were playing, waiting for my crosses! More seriously, I count myself lucky to have played with a fantastic footballer like Denis, and two more in Bobby and George. They could all do something to win any game out of nothing, so I was happy to give them the ball and let them get on with it.

RIGHT: What are two high-profile Arsenal fans doing at an Old Trafford training session, fouling me so cynically into the bargain? Comedians Mike (right) and Bernie Winters were appearing in *Babes in the Wood* at the Palace Theatre, Manchester, and Matt Busby invited them along. In fact, even though they look more familiar with rugby, both of them loved the round-ball game, appearing regularly in charity matches for the TV All-Stars. Around the mid-1960s, the worlds of football and showbiz began to overlap much more and the game became increasingly glamorised.

OPPOSITE: This was a day in the White Hart Lane sunshine that started well, took a sudden and unexpected turn for the worse and ended, in footballing terms, calamitously. It was September 1966 and, for the first time in several seasons, it seemed that Spurs were emerging as genuine title contenders. Their very canny manager, Bill Nicholson, had just bought Welsh centre-half Mike England, a terrific player who had been linked with United, and they were building up a head of steam. Hence my delight here at getting behind goalkeeper Pat Jennings to put us in front shortly before the interval.

After that we played really well, absolutely battering Spurs in their own backyard, only to be hit by an Alan Gilzean equaliser four minutes from time. After all our domination we were dismayed to have lost a point, but an even bigger shock was in store. Two minutes later Jimmy Greaves, who had not had a kick all game, sneaked in for a typically cheeky winner. We couldn't believe we were leaving London with nothing, but there was a happy ending for us – we did win the title.

ABOVE: Predictably enough, I got plenty of stick from City fans when they came to Old Trafford in September 1966 for the first Manchester derby for three years, following their recent promotion as Second Division champions. So I wasn't too dismayed when it fell to me to score this goal, the only one of the game. A cross came over from John Aston, I managed to nip past City keeper Harry Dowd and had the simple task of slipping the ball into an empty net with Alan Oakes (foreground) and Tony Book powerless to intervene.

Strangely, I had been closely involved with Harry when City had gone down in 1963. In a crucial end-of-term derby, in which we needed points to avoid relegation as desperately as City, he pulled me down unnecessarily to concede a game-changing penalty, which was converted by Albert Quixall to secure a draw.

Now, three years on, despite this setback, City were on the march again under Joe Mercer and Malcolm Allison, as we would discover to our cost in the not-too-distant future.

OPPOSITE: Here's an unusual sight in the mid-1960s – Denis Law having a dribble. In my previous life as an old fashioned up-and-down inside-forward, I had been accustomed to running with the ball, but at Manchester United Matt Busby told me to stay up front, where that crowd-pleasing art is not the way to go about the job. The fact is, if you pass the ball early and then move into space for a return, you don't need to dribble. The simple passing approach saves a lot of hassle, defenders are taken out of the equation because they have no chance to tackle and the ball covers the ground more quickly. There is no point in beating an opponent just for the sake of it.

Of course, I understand why kids love to dribble, and also that there is no finer sight in football than a mazy run by a skilful player. Bestie wasn't bad at it, but the most fantastic dribbler I've ever seen was Jimmy Johnstone of Celtic. The wee man caused more cartilage injuries to bemused defenders than anybody else on the planet. He just dipped his shoulder and he was gone, often sending team-mates the wrong way as well as the opposition. But for all that, the quickest way to beat a man is by passing – end of story.

ABOVE: Whenever fellow Aberdonian Ron Yeats and I found ourselves on the same pitch, we liked to break off from the game for a friendly chat, catch up on family news, discuss our holidays, maybe touch on politics. Or often he might thank me for the part I played in getting him to Liverpool by going round the corner from my family home to his in Printfield Walk to tell his parents that Shanks was after him. Hold on, I think I might be hallucinating here . . .

In truth, this confrontation between the colossal centre-half and myself is on the verge of turning vicious. It looks like I'm giving him a mouthful so he must have done something dreadful to upset me, because normally I was a model of decorum on the football field.

This happened in a goalless draw at Anfield in March 1967, when we were on the verge of winning our second title in three years. My team-mate David Sadler is strolling over to calm me down in his usual laid-back manner, while I might be wishing he'd hurry up and pull me away before Ron really kicks off. After all, he's a man mountain, far bigger than he looks here, where he's stooping a bit with his knees bent. Of course, there were no fatalities, and I'm sure we'd have had a drink afterwards to catch up on that Aberdeen gossip.

BELOW: A penalty kick without pressure is pretty rare in top-level football, but I have to admit that this one at West Ham in May 1967 falls into that category. United needed to win at Upton Park to clinch the title and we were three up in ten minutes, then four in front at the interval. West Ham pulled one back, but still we were cruising when I stepped up to the spot. I managed to put it away, and there was still time for me to add another goal to complete a 6-1 victory, so we could say we tied up the championship in style.

Did I have a particular method with penalties? Yes, I tried to score! Actually I aimed to keep the shot low, getting the ball as near to a post as possible. It's not foolproof, I missed a few over the years, but it's not an easy thing to do. Some guys never miss in training, but then find it a totally different proposition on a mudheap in front of 50,000 people with a major prize at stake. I usually took them for United, but occasionally I didn't feel like it if I thought I was having a bad game; then probably Bestie would take over.

Sadly, at the end of the game, there was some trouble on the terraces, but the overwhelming majority of West Ham's biggest crowd since the war were extremely generous and gave us a rousing reception. We had plenty of our own fans there, too – Manchester United have never lacked support in that part of the world.

ABOVE: Joy is unconfined in the West Ham dressing room as we toast our title in champagne. I seem to be a bit worried about my towel slipping down in front of the cameraman, which would have lowered the tone more than a little. We got bladdered on the train home from London, though we couldn't relax for the summer as we still had a game to go, at home to Stoke a week later. That turned out to be an anti-climactic goalless draw, but we showed the trophy to our fans so nobody minded.

Close pals David Sadler and George Best are standing at the back, while the cheesy grins in the front row belong to, left to right, myself, John Aston, Shay Brennan, Bill Foulkes, Tony Dunne, Paddy Crerand, Nobby Stiles and Bobby Charlton. I don't know why goalkeeper Alex Stepney was missing – maybe somebody had locked him in the loo.

CHAPTER 10

SCOTS ON TOP OF THE WORLD

ABOVE: I was all in favour of posing for this photograph during training for Scotland's game with England at Wembley in 1965 because, and I can still barely believe it, I was the tallest member of the forward line! That never happened to me either before or after, and I love looking at it even now.

Lining up in our tracksuits, left to right, are Willie Henderson, Bobby Collins, myself, Davie Wilson and Ian St John. We all look as though butter wouldn't melt in our mouths, but believe me, none of us was an angel, especially Bobby . . .

This was a time when Scotland had an abundance of terrific players to call on, an era sadly long past. There were so many exceptional performers in the mid-1960s that we could have fielded two whole teams without a perceptible weakness. That meant that top men often earned only a handful of caps, while there have been plenty of moderate players in modern times who are already into their second half-century.

ABOVE: I've just scored against England at Wembley in 1965 and my glee is obvious, but if you look closely at the expression on my face there's also a tinge of surprise. In truth the goal, which put us back in the game after being 2-0 down, was a massive fluke. I'd taken a shot from outside the box, which was extremely unusual for me. Normally, I'd be no more likely to shoot from 18 yards than 118. This was a simple strike and a fairly gentle one, which England keeper Gordon Banks saw all the way, but somehow he got in a tangle as he went down to gather it, allowing the ball to squirm into the net.

I could hardly credit that I'd scored with a hopeful poke at goal, and not even a particularly good one at that. Not that it mattered, even to such merciless mickey-takers as Paddy Crerand (left) and Willie Henderson, who are closing in to celebrate. All they cared about was that we were back in the game and there was no mention of my outrageous luck. Soon Ian St John had headed an equaliser and we ended up with a 2-2 draw, although I suppose I ought to point out that it was against nine fit men, as Ray Wilson had gone off injured and Johnny Byrne was a limping passenger. Still, it doesn't mention that in the record books.

ABOVE: All the fire and the passion and the rampant will to win that typifies contests between England and Scotland are captured in this wonderful picture. England keeper Gordon Banks has surely won the race for the ball, but I'm still giving it everything, going for the kill, ready to pounce at high velocity if he makes a rare fumble. In fact, he scooped up the ball and dived out of my way, which was a good job, or he might have landed in the back of the stand. I still don't know how I missed him! Behind me, perhaps expecting to pick up the pieces from a seemingly inevitable collision, is Rangers winger Davie Wilson. Also appearing on the scene is Jack Charlton, who was winning his first cap (along with Nobby Stiles), while George Cohen and Johnny Byrne are in the background on the left.

BOBBY CHARLTON:

This is the friendliest Denis has looked all afternoon! He ought to be pleased, because he has just scored as Scotland came back from two down to draw. He was never above clattering me when we met in internationals, but there were no hard feelings.

OPPOSITE: At the end of a spring afternoon of frantic, often dramatic action between England and Scotland at Wembley, Bobby Charlton and I swap our sweaty shirts. I've no idea what's happened to Bobby's, I must have given it away. I wonder if he's still got mine.

I never found it a problem to play against clubmates in international games. For that 90 minutes I think of them as foreigners, not friends I hope to be celebrating with in our next game at Old Trafford. They're the opposition, the enemy if you like, and I'll do anything to beat them. Certainly, the likes of Bobby and Nobby Stiles understood that, and I don't believe they'd have wanted it any other way. It was the same with Ray Wilson when we were at Huddersfield together – club loyalties were suspended absolutely.

Is there ribbing between clubmates before an international? There might be a bit from Bobby or Nobby, but not from me. I was more serious! Don't forget that usually Scotland were the underdogs, so I needed total concentration on the job if I was going to help my country get the right result.

On a less fractious note, the two goalkeepers – Bill Brown of Scotland (left) and England's Gordon Banks – are watching us make the exchange. I wonder if they swapped jerseys, too.

LEFT: This was probably the best goal I ever scored for Scotland. It came against England at Hampden Park in April 1966, just a few months before they became world champions, and it was a crisp near-post header from a Willie Johnston corner just before half time. It felt like an important moment, too, because we were two down at the time and this put us back into contention. Unfortunately, we lost 4-3 at the end of a ding-dong battle, but it turned out we scored as many goals against England that afternoon as they would concede in the whole of that summer's World Cup tournament.

As Willie took the kick, I was darting around trying to lose my marker, Bobby Moore, at the last possible split-second. He was a very fair opponent so I knew there would be nothing underhand and I could concentrate solely on the flight of the ball. Bobby was good in the air and he read the game brilliantly, but on this occasion I must have anticipated a little better than he did.

Just look at that vast bank of humanity at the other end of the pitch. Even after all these years, the sight of it, the very thought of it, takes my breath away.

OPPOSITE: I was so proud to wear that beautiful, pure Scotland shirt with no mark on it except the badge, and never more so than on this blessed day at Wembley in May 1967 when we became undisputed champions of the world – well, nobody was arguing north of the border.

ABOVE: Could there be any greater motivation for a hot-blooded Scot than playing at Wembley against the 'Auld Enemy', who also happened to be the world champions, a team that had not been beaten since they had lifted the Jules Rimet Trophy on that same turf some nine months earlier? No, I really don't think so.

We played very well that day, richly deserving our 3-2 win, and I was delighted to score the opener, although this wasn't it. Here, with Martin Peters in attendance but not close enough to make a tackle, I've attempted a left-foot volley, probably from a cross by right winger Jimmy Johnstone. I can't recall how close it went, but it must have been a near thing because there's Alex Ferguson on his feet in the back of the stand!

As Fergie said when he took over at Manchester United, he wanted to knock Liverpool off their ******* perch. Well, we felt exactly the same about England.

ABOVE: Considering that I've just put Scotland in front against England on their own pitch in what was described by some excitable observers as the most momentous clash ever between our two countries, my face is not registering my customary unrestrained emotion. My only explanation is that it must have taken a few moments for it to sink in that I had scored in such a massive match.

It happened just before the half-hour when Willie Wallace shot and, knowing he was such a terrific striker of the ball, I gambled that Gordon Banks might not be able to hold it. I was on the spot to prod in the rebound. There's Martin Peters again, behind the fallen Banks, once more a little too late to make a meaningful challenge.

ABOVE: I think Nobby Stiles has just accidentally nicked the ball away while attempting to scythe me down from behind during Scotland's win at Wembley in the spring of 1967 – don't worry, I'm only joking. The little fella from Collyhurst might have mistimed an occasional challenge, but essentially he was very fair and a far more accomplished footballer than most people realised. For instance, he read the game as well as anybody I ever encountered and he was a lovely passer, too.

I'm pretty sure that Gordon Banks and I crashed into each other here, but I didn't get a penalty. With Nobby sliding in, I might have become the meat in a sandwich. Clearly I haven't got control of the ball, but if he's robbed me with his left foot it's truly incredible, because normally he used that only for standing on.

Given the ferocity of his tackling, it's amazing that Nobby wasn't wearing shinpads in such an ultra-competitive contest. Often he used to start with them, but then discard them because they were uncomfortable.

In the course of an England–Scotland game, Bobby Charlton and I wouldn't run into each other too often, but certainly I'd have put my foot in if he came close with the ball. Probably he took care not to have it when I was anywhere in the vicinity!

NOBBY STILES:

Denis was only slightly built, really there wasn't much of him at all, but he was fearsomely brave and he had an amazing aura about him, a presence that was absolutely unique. People just couldn't take their eyes off him. I've never seen anything like Denis in the air – he would seem to hang there, then his head would snap back and the ball would flash into the net before his markers could move.

LEFT: The game was at Wembley but it felt like Hampden, there was so much noise. This lad seems quite pleased with our 3-2 victory. I'm not sure who he was, but he might be Alex Ferguson's brother! Whoever he is, he almost throttled me with one hand while waving his tam-o'-shanter at the heavens with the other. If he's still around I hope he sees his picture in the book – and I hope he buys it! I'm sorry to say I didn't have a clue what he was saying to me, but I'm sure it was colourful. He wasn't asking for the latest cricket score, that's for certain.

So many of these marvellous fans used to save up for two years to make the trip to London. You've heard of a Christmas club, well this was a Wembley club. That's why I felt such a huge obligation to them. Of course, they headed south with huge expectations. This time we managed to meet them, and I was delighted to join in with their celebrations. Scottish supporters are as good as any, wherever in the world they go, and they've suffered a lot through the years.

Was I uneasy with this guy hanging round my neck? Not in the least. It was all part and parcel of the day and I was just pleased to share his happiness, which is emphasised by the glum figure of Greavsie behind us. Mind, if the date had been 1961 instead of 1967, then I might have been worried. I'd have been looking for the rope in his hand!

OPPOSITE: Scotland training camps were not all hard graft, and when we were at Largs most of us enjoyed a round at the small golf club just along the road. Here I don't seem over-impressed by Billy Bremner's swing, although to be fair it doesn't look half bad and didn't deserve my disparaging comments. But most of us were wind-up merchants, and you can bet your life that Willie Henderson (right) would have been joining in. At least, I think that's Willie, or is it someone wearing one of those ridiculous sets of false nose, false glasses and false moustache? It's hard to believe that anybody would choose to go out looking like that!

Both these two boys were tremendous footballers, and Billy was an inspirational captain, too. We had some fiery battles at club level, but the fact that he was Leeds and I was Manchester United made no difference on these occasions. We were there for Scotland, and that's all that mattered.

ABOVE: Sometimes it's just too painful to look, but if I'd been a little braver when Northern Ireland's Johnny Crossan took this penalty at Windsor Park, Belfast, in October 1967 I'd have seen Ronnie Simpson, our keeper, pull off a fine diving save. Sadly, it didn't make much difference in the end because we lost 1-0, which was abysmally disappointing as it was a European Championship qualifier, and after beating England we had been on a high.

At least it got Johnny off the hook for failing to score from the spot, though, and he's a good lad. Once, when the Troubles were very bad, we went to Belfast together to make a presentation and I was pretty nervous about the whole trip. When we got to the pub I walked in first and there was this dreadful, ominous silence. But when they caught sight of Johnny behind me, the atmosphere changed completely and we had a great night. Still, I had the uncomfortable feeling that if I'd been on my own, I'd have had real problems.

One of the great pities about the ditching of the Home International Championship was that it took away from the people of Ireland a much-needed diversion from the sectarian trauma that tainted their daily lives. Now the political situation is more tranquil (fingers crossed), I'd like to see the tournament restored to the football calendar.

CHAPTER 11

DESCENDING FROM THE SUMMIT

ABOVE: Why are Spurs skipper Dave Mackay and I looking so cheerful as we brandish the Charity Shield in the home dressing room at Old Trafford in August 1967, while the fellas behind us – Bill Foulkes (left), debutant Brian Kidd and United chairman Louis Edwards – all appear so grim? Maybe because Dave, a great mate of mine from playing for Scotland together down the years, had arranged for us to have a pint or three of McEwan's, and he hadn't invited them.

Dave was one of the most competitive people I've ever met, and a born leader. Even in training he had to win at everything, whether it was a five-a-side, a race or an impromptu game of flicking a penny from boot to head to shoulder. Then when the game began he would stick out that barrel chest and be ready to take on the world.

When I was at Huddersfield, he was one of the main reasons I fancied joining Spurs. They were so glamorous,

MATT BUSBY:

Injury nagged at Denis . . . he suffered it stoically for a long time. There were people who thought he was laying it on a bit . . . but it was eventually discovered that a piece of cartilage had caused him absolute agony. He overcame it all, and if he never quite reached his old heights, he still fought back to play for Scotland again, which is high enough for most people.

ABOVE: 'Where does it hurt, Denis?' It is early in 1968 and I'm discussing my worsening knee problem with Matt Busby. Although I could still pass comfortably with the outside of my foot or my instep, as soon as I turned my knee, opening the joint to use the inside of my foot, then I felt a sharp pain. I'm demonstrating this to the Boss and he's looking worried, no doubt knowing the likely outcome. Sure enough, although I managed to play in the first leg of the European Cup semi-final against Real Madrid, I missed the second leg and, worst of all, I missed the final with Benfica at Wembley.

with other wonderful players such as Danny Blanchflower, John White, Cliff Jones and Bill Brown, and I was very much attracted to London. That's where it all happened, wasn't it?

We shared this Charity Shield after an entertaining 3-3 draw, best remembered for Pat Jennings scoring with a goal-kick past our keeper Alex Stepney. Poor old Steppers, we don't let him forget that even today!

DAVE MACKAY:

Denis was good and he knew it, but he wasn't big-headed in any way. He was a cheeky chappie who could see the fun in everything and his general good humour and mischievousness were infectious. We became pals straight away. I wasn't surprised when he became one of the most admired forwards of his generation and one of the greatest Scottish footballers ever.

It's fair to say that when my Scotland team-mate Ian Ure visited Old Trafford with Arsenal in October 1967, we did not spend the afternoon exchanging pleasantries. I managed to lose him for this header ABOVE and felt I was having a decent game, but for some reason he clattered me a few times and at first I tried to be reasonable. 'Excuse me, Ian old bean, do you think you could stop kicking me, please?' Or words to that effect. But in the end I snapped. He caught me once too often and I threw a punch at him. Sadly, from my point of view at the time, I missed, but unfortunately it happened right under the referee's nose and we were both sent off.

Ure looks angry here RIGHT, with his fist clenched, but he should have been happy because my punch had just whistled past that jutting chin of his. The trouble was, he was massive so I could hardly reach him. For me it was the old story: I get fouled repeatedly, I issue a warning, I get whacked again and I retaliate. After that, it wasn't much use telling the referee that he started it ABOVE RIGHT. It was a slice of drama played out in front of this huge audience who had come to watch a game of football, and I suppose it was disgraceful really.

We didn't make up with a drink after the game, and I was surprised when United signed him the following year. In my opinion, he wasn't the greatest. He was six-foot something but when he jumped to head the ball he seemed like he was five-foot eight! I don't think it was one of the best signings United ever made. When he retired he became a prison warder in Scotland.

ABOVE: When you take off like this and manage to catch the ball just right, so it ends up in the back of the net, you do expect a goal for your pains. So you might say I was a teeny bit miffed when the referee ruled out this effort against Spurs at Old Trafford in September 1967. Why? Search me. Apparently, he blew for offside, but how could that be with keeper Pat Jennings, Phil Beal and another defender between me and the goal? And it couldn't have been for dangerous kicking because there's nobody near me. The camera doesn't lie – this was a blatant mistake by an official who was perfectly placed to witness what happened.

You didn't see many overheads in those days, but I was always ready to try anything to reach a cross. If the ball was played in

behind me and I couldn't meet it by conventional means, then rather than let it go I would just launch myself. Sometimes I'd end up looking daft; on other occasions the ball might creep across the line. Certainly I never tried to direct it to a corner of the net, I just wanted to hit the general target. If I didn't know exactly where it was going, what chance did the keeper have?

I suffered another black moment in this game when I missed a penalty, but happily we won 3-1, and that after Alan Gilzean had put Spurs in front in the first minute. George Best equalised soon afterwards, then I finally scored with a late header and Bestie rounded it off with his second.

ABOVE: Like a batsman stroking the perfect cover drive from the meat of his bat, sometimes a striker can score a goal that brings a feeling of comprehensive satisfaction, and this effort against Sheffield United at Old Trafford in April 1968 falls into that category. Brian Kidd has delivered his cross slightly low so I have had to reach forward, but I have met it with the centre of my forehead and it's gone into the net like a bullet. On this occasion, my timing is absolutely right. If I'd jumped a split second earlier or later, almost certainly I wouldn't have scored. It was a sweet moment, especially as it was the only goal of the game.

ABOVE: This speaks eloquently to me of a bygone era. It's February 1968 and the scene is Turf Moor, Burnley. Look at the old-fashioned stand with the pillar obstructing the view; the ranks of standing fans packed in shoulder to shoulder, many of them in the open air; and the terraces of houses overlooking the pitch. This was when football was the people's game, and they lived close to it.

Here I'm giving George Best a cuddle after he'd put us in front and seemingly on the way to extending our 12-game unbeaten run, but Burnley was always a hard place to go and they fought back to win through goals by Brian O'Neil and Martin Dobson. This was exactly the type of tough encounter on a cold afternoon that you needed to win to lift the title. We didn't and, duly, we lost our championship crown, too.

ABOVE: Ever since before I became a professional footballer, Francisco Gento had been a hero to me. Now I was Manchester United captain, he was skipper of the legendary Real Madrid, and here we were shaking hands before the first leg of our European Cup semi-final at Old Trafford in April 1968. It was amazing to think that he had faced United in their first European Cup semi, all of 11 years earlier. Though by now in his mid-thirties, 'Paco' could still move like an express train and I had no doubts that he remained a major threat. I already knew him personally, as we had played together for the Rest of the World back in 1963, and it was tremendous to meet up with him again, especially on such an important occasion.

I didn't realise it at the time, but the referee is Tofiq Bakhramov, best known as the Russian linesman who gave the nod to Geoff Hurst's crucial and hugely controversial second goal against West Germany in the World Cup final of 1966, when his shot crashed against the crossbar and bounced down. I should have asked him if that ball had really crossed the line. If he'd said 'yes', then perhaps I should have advised him to acquire a pair of spectacles and to give up refereeing!

OPPOSITE: I don't want to make excuses, but when Real Madrid visited Old Trafford, I was far from fully fit. We didn't have a big squad in those days and so I played. It was pretty painful to push off my right knee when I jumped for a header, which might explain my expression here, although I might just have been puffing with the exertion. Anyway, I've missed the ball, and I'm leaning on the Real defender, giving John Aston the chance of a clear contact. Unfortunately, it's come to him at an awkward angle, catching him high and to the side rather than flush on the forehead, and the opportunity has slipped away. We won 1-0 thanks to a terrific goal from George Best, but that seemed a slender lead to take to the Bernabeu.

By the time of the second encounter, I had no chance of playing, and was absolutely gutted as I watched us go 3-1 down on the night. They were in total command, but then they got cocky and sat back, allowing David Sadler to score a scruffy goal that put us level on aggregate. Finally our big, old centre-half Bill Foulkes, of all the unlikely people, strode forward to slot in a brilliant goal to seal our aggregate victory, and Manchester United were in the European Cup final.

ABOVE: Sitting between Nobby Stiles and Matt Busby – and tantalisingly close to the European Cup, which I didn't have the honour of holding up at Wembley – I've got the biggest grin of the lot. Although I missed out on the climax against Benfica, I like to think that I contributed in the earlier rounds, and I believed that I was young enough, in my prime at 28, to be part of a United side that would go on to win it again. That said, I did worry that my knee trouble would seriously impair my future.

If I had my time over again, I wouldn't have played in several games. I would have insisted that I wait until I recovered. Modern technology hadn't arrived at that stage and I wasn't the only one struggling, with Nobby, George Best and John Fitzpatrick all suffering from long-term knee problems. People often ask why that team declined so rapidly after '68, and maybe this furnishes a clue. Still, I was confident there was still fuel in our collective tank. Critics talk about our ageing squad, but Bill Foulkes was the only real veteran. Surely we'd do it again, wouldn't we?

Left to right, back row: Bill Foulkes, John Aston, Jimmy Rimmer, Alex Stepney, Alan Gowling, David Herd. Middle row: David Sadler, Tony Dunne, Shay Brennan, Paddy Crerand, George Best, Francis Burns, trainer Jack Crompton. Front row: Jim Ryan, Nobby Stiles, myself, Matt Busby, Bobby Charlton, Brian Kidd, John Fitzpatrick.

NOBBY STILES:

After all Denis achieved for United, it was a crying shame that he was forced to miss the 1968 European Cup final through injury. He deserved to be in the team that night at Wembley; it would have been his ultimate coronation. Off the pitch as well as on it, there was always a sparkle about Denis. He was fantastic company and one of the nicest fellas you could ever wish to meet.

ABOVE: Just look at George here, absolutely fantastic in the full bloom of youth, a really handsome boy. Love the wig, too!

I had a wonderful rapport with Bestie, though he could be a bit difficult to play with. He was like wee Jimmy Johnstone in that respect. You would run into great positions and call for the ball, then you didn't get it and it could make you mad. But then George would drop his shoulder yet again, go past another posse of defenders and score a sensational goal – so what could you say?

Funnily enough, we became better friends after we'd finished playing. Although there was only six years' difference in our ages, we were kind of from different generations. I had a family and responsibilities, while he was single and floating about. It was the Swinging Sixties and he was the fifth Beatle, but there was no way the rest of us were envious of him . . . officially! But by the time we'd retired the age gap didn't matter. When you're 18 and 24, there's a big difference. But when you're 33 and 39, there's no gap at all.

GEORGE BEST:

Denis Law was a magnificent footballer and he's a tremendous human being. Certainly he was one of the most exciting performers I have ever played with or against, and I consider myself lucky to count him among the best, and most enduring, of the friends I made in the game. Denis offered the fans such fabulous value for money, and I understand completely why they loved him so much.

OPPOSITE: I'm playing the cool, mature, elder statesman here during a break in play against Queens Park Rangers at Loftus Road in October 1968, obviously telling one of my more hot-tempered team-mates to calm down. What's that? Do I hear somebody snorting derision, or maybe shouting the words 'pot' and 'kettle' in my direction? Come on, surely not! I've no idea who I was talking to, Paddy Crerand probably, although there were one or two other candidates. Whatever, Rangers' Tony Hazell looks totally unimpressed by my diplomatic skills.

At first glance I was surprised that I appeared to be wearing shinguards, which I hated, but on closer examination I can just about discern a bandage pad under my right sock.

ABOVE: I'm in the back of Liverpool's net but more importantly so is the ball, although it's out of shot, presumably nestling in the far bottom corner. Keeper Tommy Lawrence is on his backside, appealing that the goal should be disallowed and urging the referee to consult his linesman. I've got a slightly anxious expression on my face – or is it guilt? – but the goal stood, which was enough to give us victory in this tight encounter at Old Trafford in December 1968.

Tommy was a typical goalkeeper, by which I mean stark, staring bonkers. Most of them are; they have to be to do that job. Actually, he was a lovely fella and a tremendous operator who read the game really well, frequently leaving his line to mop up danger, which is why he was one of the first to be called a sweeper-keeper. He was born in Warrington, but played for Scotland a couple of times, so he was one of us really.

ABOVE: It's like a battlefield at St James' Park in April 1969, and cynical observers might contend that I only chased back to our penalty box to join in the rumpus. I prefer to say that the picture just goes to prove that I was willing to do my bit in defence, even if I didn't make a habit of it.

It looks as though the big Welshman Wyn Davies, who was later to serve both Manchester clubs, is acting as peacemaker here, but I can't believe I was about to fight Nobby Stiles! Our keeper Jimmy Rimmer is laid out, still clutching the ball, while Newcastle forward Arthur Horsfield is rolling around in agony. Meanwhile my team-mate John Fitzpatrick obviously knows my reputation, so he's intent on restraining me. I'd guess that Nobby was claiming for a foul on Jimmy, while Newcastle wanted a penalty. We lost 2-0 and certainly one of their goals was from the spot, put away by Pop Robson.

At the time, both clubs had made it to European semi-finals, us in the European Cup and the Magpies in the Fairs Cup, which they went on to win. They were a decent side, and I loved playing up there because their passionate fans always created such a cracking atmosphere.

ABOVE: I was lucky enough to have a fabulous rapport with the Stretford End, and it was a relationship I treasured, but I didn't want to milk it so it was very rare for me to run to them as I did here after scoring against Newcastle in September 1968. I must admit the goal is hazy in my memory, but the records show that I had just found the net from 30 yards. Me, hit a shot from 30 yards? I wonder if there was a misprint and it should have been three! If it really happened, it must have been a freak, maybe taking three or four deflections on the way in. Clearly the Newcastle keeper Iam McFaul is just as flabbergasted as me. I must have run a long way to celebrate and he hasn't even retrieved the ball from the net. I can feel plenty of sympathy for the poor fella.

ABOVE: I don't know why John Fitzpatrick and I are looking so chirpy on our way back from Milan in April 1969 because we had just been beaten 2-0 by AC in the first leg of the European Cup semi-final, and my fellow Aberdonian, who appears to be guarding his duty-free with his life, had been sent off for kicking the Swedish winger Kurt Hamrin. My only explanation is that I've had a couple of drinks and Fitz has got severe wind.

Actually, far more likely is that we were being entertained by the fellow at the back, the supremely talented *Times* football correspondent Geoffrey Green, now sadly no longer with us. He was a brilliant writer and absolutely wonderful company and, boy, could he drink! I think it's unlikely that that's a glass of water in his hand. Here he looks almost like a ghost that has appeared on the negative. That's the explanation! We're hearing this other-worldly voice and we're laughing nervously ...

OPPOSITE TOP: This is the moment when I shall always believe United were robbed of a place in their second successive European Cup final, and I was unfairly deprived of my only opportunity to take part in club football's grandest occasion. We were two goals down when we started the second leg against AC Milan on a tumultuous night at Old Trafford, where the atmosphere was absolutely boiling. Bobby Charlton pulled one back with 20 minutes to go and then I was so positive that I had scored the equaliser, scrambling the ball home after a chip by Paddy Crerand, that here I turn away to celebrate. I swear it had crossed the line by a mile before it was scooped away by a defender, and the referee was well placed to see it, but for some reason he didn't give us the goal and we went out. Had it gone to 2-0, we would have beaten them for sure, so we felt a sharp sense of injustice but there was nothing we could do about it.

I had been marked by my old Torino mate, Rosato. He kicked me incessantly and eventually, after warning him of the consequences if he persisted, I swung round and whacked him so hard with my fist that he lost all his front teeth. I felt terrible about that and apologised afterwards, but he didn't hold a grudge. After all, he was in the European Cup final and I wasn't.

LEFT: Foiled by keeper Alberto Poletti in an attempt to score against the dirtiest team I've ever known. This was the Old Trafford second leg of our World Club Championship clash with Estudiantes of La Plata, who included some thugs who seemed prepared to sink to any depths to win the trophy. We lost 1-0 in Argentina in a game that was no better than a bloodbath. They kicked and scratched and bit, pulled every low-down trick in the book, and they got away with it. The referee gave us little protection from their brutal tactics, then sent off Nobby Stiles for gesticulating.

In Manchester the contest was considerably cleaner, because they couldn't have got away with such outrageous behaviour over here, but still they were far from being angels. They took an early lead, and although Willie Morgan managed a late equaliser on the night, we never looked like winning. The whole thing was an utter scandal. I don't know if the Mafia play football, but if they do, this is what it must be like.

ABOVE: I suppose nothing is impossible, but here's an achievement it's difficult to imagine being repeated any time soon – three players from one club being fêted as European Footballer of the Year. I guess it might conceivably be on for Barcelona, with the likes of Messi, Iniesta, Xavi and company in their ranks, but still the likelihood is remote.

This is George Best receiving his 1968 award from journalist Max Urbini (left) of *France Football*. Bobby Charlton got his in 1966 and mine arrived in 1964, and the short time-span makes it even more remarkable. I think the proudest man on the pitch is Matt Busby, especially as two of the winners rose through the junior ranks at United, and he had known me throughout my entire career. Probably, too, he thought back to the lads who died at Munich, wondering if Duncan Edwards might have been similarly honoured had he lived.

At the time I didn't appreciate how amazing it all was, but rather took it for granted. Looking back, I wish I'd savoured it more at the time.

BOBBY CHARLTON:

Denis is right to make the point about Duncan. If he'd been spared, I believe he'd have won everything it was possible to win.

ABOVE: This looks like a serious goal celebration to me. No histrionics, just the recognition that we had scored when we badly needed to, when we were in a tough situation. On the other hand, I might just have been saying to George: 'I'll see you in the bar later on. Crerand's getting them in!'

George and I weren't best buddies at the time, but there was always a certain closeness between us that neither of us had with Bobby Charlton. I became much closer to Bobby later on. When he was playing, it was as though he was responsible for the behaviour of the team, and it could make him appear a bit stiff. After all, he'd been through Munich, and if he saw someone taking liberties, it offended him. And looking back now, I don't blame him.

ABOVE: 'What the hell are you doing here? I can't believe it.' If that's not exactly what I'm saying as I shake hands with new United arrival Ian Ure at the training ground in August 1969, then certainly it's what I'm thinking. It's in Bestie's mind, too. Everybody's smiling, but I think they were a bit bemused that the Arsenal centre-half I had scrapped with not so long ago was now coming to help us out of a sequence of bad results. To be fair, even Ure himself is looking a tad rueful, as though he recognised the irony of the situation.

Ian and I had been pals in the Scotland team and he'd come as a strong man in the centre of defence. He wasn't the worst player in the world, but I didn't think he was anything like an adequate replacement for Bill Foulkes (left). Joining in the merriment are, left to right, George Best, Paddy Crerand, John Fitzpatrick, Ian Ure, Willie Morgan and myself. Meanwhile new chief coach Wilf McGuinness (right) looks as if he hasn't a clue what's going on.

WILF McGUINNESS:

I know exactly what's happening here. Denis is looking at Ian Ure's hand to see if his knuckles had healed up!

OPPOSITE: Clutching my sleeves was a habit of mine; I always felt comfortable with something to hold on to. Also it was very convenient for wiping my nose. After a while the material got hard, and was very handy if I wanted to give someone a crack. I shouldn't be saying this really, it's supposed to be a family book.

ABOVE: I've just scored for United in a semi-final against Manchester City at Old Trafford, but somehow my celebration is less than ecstatic. Perhaps it's because it was in the League Cup, a competition that never seemed to have the stature of others. That said, it would have been great to win it at a time we weren't in danger of lifting any other silverware, and there was no way we went out to get beat.

After City won the first leg 2-1 at Maine Road, this goal made it 2-1 to us on the night, 3-3 on aggregate. After that, we mounted waves of pressure but then City scored a bizarre winner. Francis Lee blasted an indirect free-kick and if Alex Stepney had simply let it go in, it wouldn't have counted. But his immediate reaction was to parry the shot, which kept the ball live and Mike Summerbee poked in the winner. You couldn't really blame Steppers because keepers are pro-grammed to make saves and that's what he did.

At this point City, with the likes of Mike, Franny and Colin Bell in their prime, were a very fine team, undoubtedly their best in modern times.

OPPOSITE: Who me? You've got to be joking. I wasn't even in the box – and even if I was, I never touched the keeper! Obviously I'm the subject of a false accusation and am morti-fied, protesting my innocence and wondering why anyone should ever have dreamed that I committed an offence. How dare they suggest that I might have transgressed?

On the other hand, perhaps I'm suffering from a touch of indigestion and am looking for a bit of sympathy.

OPPOSITE: This is a classic picture of a couple of well-toned lads – one maybe a tiny bit older than the other – training in pre-season at the Cliff. We didn't look too bad, did we? George was a bit browner than me, but both of us had our six-packs and essentially we were in great nick. We weren't racing each other; rather we were posing for the cameras, a bit of beefcake for the newspapers. Just look at that co-ordination. That's what I call synchronised running. Mind, it took us hours to get the choreography just right!

ABOVE: There was something supremely satisfying about pulling on that rich, red shirt. I must admit the barnet has grown a bit long here, back in the summer of 1971, and the sideburns make me look as though I'm auditioning for a part in *Poldark*! But I'm looking good – I just wish I looked like that now. How often have I said that in this book? I'm in danger of getting maudlin in my old age.

CHAPTER 12

NO WAY
TO SAY
GOODBYE

ABOVE: 'What's your dad like? He's my new boss.' That might have been the gist of my remarks to these young O'Farrells after their father, Frank, had taken over as manager of Manchester United in the summer of 1971. Paddy Crerand and I met the family, including Frank's wife Ann, in the canteen at our Cliff training ground, and it was all very friendly. Sadly, the players' relationship with our new gaffer never really got off the ground.

The team made a bright start, topping the league table in the autumn, but we never gelled properly and results fell away disastrously in the new year. Why? Frank was never close to the players, we hardly ever saw him, and when we did we felt he was not a great communicator. I said at the time that he came a stranger and left a stranger, and that sums it up. In the end his sacking, in December 1972, with United bottom of the table, was inevitable.

OPPOSITE: A study in total concentration as I change direction, attempting to go round an opponent without getting too close. At this moment, all that exists for me is the mechanics of the game. The crowd could be chanting that my house was on fire and I wouldn't hear them.

ABOVE: George Best was flying in the autumn of 1971 and, for a brief period under Frank O'Farrell, so were United as we stormed to the top of the First Division. Here George completes his hat-trick in an exhilarating 4-2 win over West Ham at Old Trafford, with Alan Gowling (No 4) and me looking on in admiration. It's going too far to say that George carried the team at this point – no one man can do that – but certainly his influence was colossal. It was a shame that everything fell apart for Frank, George and United so soon afterwards. Even when we were heading the table, critics such as Malcolm Allison and Brian Clough insisted that we were a bad team, and I'm sorry to say that certainly we weren't the team we had been.

ABOVE: I'm practically turning myself inside out to evade this challenge from Phil Hoadley of Crystal Palace at Selhurst Park in September 1971, but it was worth the effort because the ball ended up in the net. When you're attempting to pull off a volley with a defender virtually in your shorts, you need a bit of luck. I just tried to hit the target – never mind top corner or bottom corner, as long as I managed to whack the ball in the right general direction I was happy. In fact, often a miscue was more effective than a sweet connection because nobody knew where the ball was going.

What amazes me about this picture is the number of girls in the crowd. I've never seen so many. The pity is, they wouldn't have been there to watch me – they'd have been ogling Bestie, seen here on the right being closely marked by Mel Blyth. The Palace man on the left is David Payne.

ABOVE: It's the same sunny day at the Palace and here I'm celebrating one of my two goals in a 3-1 victory. This is a picture
that has been rather widely used down the years, but I have no
hesitation in rolling it out again because it does capture the
moment pretty effectively. The designer of this book's cover
liked it anyway.

The player in the background is Bobby Tambling, who
made a tremendous success of the unenviable task of replacing
the incomparable Jimmy Greaves as Chelsea's goalscorer-in-chief
before putting in a more than decent shift for Palace towards the
end of his career.

OPPOSITE: Amid the tumult of Manchester United's First Division clash with Fulham at Craven Cottage in the early 1970s, there was still time for a bit of light relief. Often we found time for a joke in those days, whereas it all seems so desperately, deadly serious in the Premier League era. I like to think the way we approached the game was rather more enlightened. Some of us were old enough to remember the war, and we could contrast those days with our own living conditions, which we thought were pretty good. We were making a few quid, we could look after our families and have some fun – what more could we want? Certainly, we tried to win every match, but if we didn't then it wasn't the end of the world. It was a game, we had it in perspective and human relationships were important. For instance, it was great to meet up again with the fellow in the background, Stan Horne, who was in digs with me during my first stay at Manchester City.

What am I saying here? Well, I might be making a rueful remark about missing an easy chance, or maybe I was informing my marker that his most recent tackle was on the strong side. 'Please accept this as a first warning. I wouldn't do that again ...'

ABOVE: The Kop had been crowing because we were two down at Anfield in September 1971 but, admittedly just for a fleeting moment, the roar subsided as this goal put United back in the game. Bestie (far left) hared down the right wing and cracked the ball over very hard, about a yard off the ground, and I was fortunate enough to direct it into the net with the side of my foot. To be honest I couldn't miss, and Emlyn Hughes, Larry Lloyd and keeper Ray Clemence were helpless to intervene.

Later, Bobby Charlton equalised with one of his trademark scorchers from the corner of the box, so we were more than happy to go home with a point after being two adrift. Probably we'd have been happy enough to take a point at Anfield if we'd been two up!

I loved playing there because the atmosphere was always crackling and Liverpool were never less than formidable opponents. If you wanted to test yourself under extreme pressure, there was no better place.

ABOVE: Of course, I didn't kick him, ref. I'm as innocent as the driven snow. I'm hurt that it could even cross your mind that I'd resort to violence. Actually, all these years later, I'm beginning to be a wee bit embarrassed by this recurring theme . . .

OPPOSITE: Accepting a wigging from referee Roger Kirkpatrick during a 2-0 defeat at White Hart Lane in the spring of 1972. This was our seventh successive league reverse and, from leading the table, we had slumped hopelessly out of contention for the title. Small wonder, then, that I was feeling the strain.

Kirkpatrick was something of a character, extremely talkative and reminiscent of Mr Pickwick with his round face and his sideburns. You never see refs that shape any more, but he was a decent official; you could always have a dialogue with him, although I feel the really good referees were the ones you didn't notice.

I appreciate that the guy in charge of any game has an immensely difficult job. I'm going to be only one of 22 people who might be rabbiting at him and he's got to keep a lid on everything while doing his best to make the right decisions. I know it might be said that I caused more problems than most, but I think that, within reason, a bit of by-play is all part of the entertainment.

ABOVE: Ouch! I can almost hear my old bones creaking as I begin to pull myself to my feet in our FA Cup tie with Middlesbrough at Old Trafford in February 1972. Clearly at this point, a combination of injuries and old age was taking its toll. If the picture was taken towards the end of the game, it wouldn't have been so bad. But if it was near the beginning, then I was in trouble.

ABOVE: I can't decide whether I'm adopting a pose to model United's new kit ahead of the 1972-73 season, or my back's gone again and I simply can't climb to my feet.

This was one of my favourite shirts, with the badge on the chest and a white collar that reminded me of my old Torino top. When I ran on to the pitch wearing this, it made me feel ten feet tall; I'd be brimming with confidence. Mind, that season, which turned out to be my last at Old Trafford, we only just managed to avoid relegation, experiencing the same sort of narrow squeak that we'd had in my first at the club a decade earlier.

After we'd won the European Cup I think one or two players, without mentioning names, should have been replaced. Many of us were still in our prime, and if the changes had been made, I believe we could have been successful for a few more years.

ABOVE: Old Trafford is looking its best, packed to the rafters on the first day of a new season, but – and I'm adapting Bobby Charlton's immortal description here – if the theatre is spick and span, then sadly the dreams are of the nightmare variety. We lost 2-1 to Ipswich on 12 August 1972 to begin a campaign of serial travail, and this picture aptly encapsulates our frustration.

Willie Morgan (right) has shot at goal but the referee is blowing for offside and it looks like I'm the offender. Behind

me is young Brian Kidd, who should have been looking forward to a decade as a top man for Manchester United, but who instead was soon to leave the club, surely unfulfilled despite the European Cup winner's medal he had earned on his 19th birthday. Still, he went on to enjoy a terrific career with a succession of leading clubs, and later made magnificent contributions to both United and City as a coach.

BRIAN KIDD:

Denis Law was my idol when I arrived at Old Trafford. He was so charismatic, especially on the great European nights. The bigger the stage, the better, for Denis. He always seemed to rise to the occasion. It was like watching the heavyweight champion of the world.

ABOVE: When new Manchester United manager Tommy Docherty brought in a succession of fellow Scots during 1972-73, the press labelled them Doc's Tartan Army, but I'd suggest they went a mile too far when they set up Paddy Crerand with some bagpipes. Was Paddy a musician? Absolutely not. He had no sense of rhythm whatsoever. He wouldn't even know if he had the pipes the right way up, and I'd guess he'd be blowing down the wrong one, for sure. I'm all for scaring the English half to death, but this was plain ridiculous.

Having the good grace to look slightly embarrassed are, left to right, Alex Forsyth, Martin Buchan, George Graham, the Doc himself, me, John Fitzpatrick and Willie Morgan.

PADDY CRERAND:

You tell me any sensible person who knows one end of the bagpipes from the other! Tommy Docherty could have played them okay, because he was always full of wind. If he told me it was sunny outside, I'd go out and check the weather.

ABOVE: Putting the world to rights in the dressing room with new Manchester United boss Tommy Docherty and centre-half David Sadler. Sir Matt Busby consulted me about the appointment of the Doc because only recently I'd been playing under him for Scotland. I knew him both as a manager and a player; I rated him highly and so, at the time, I was pleased with his arrival.

Perhaps oddly for a man who espoused skill and class, he never really embraced Saddy, who was a particularly stylish operator, although if you wanted to be really picky you might say he lacked a bit of naughtiness that might have given him an extra edge.

Of course, the Doc was appointed to reshape the team; he inherited the high-quality Martin Buchan and effectively replaced David with Jim Holton, a much more physical type. Whether anyone agreed with him or not, he had to make his own choice. Here he's looking thoughtful, as though he's already contemplating the need for change.

DAVID SADLER:

These were testing times at United, and the Doc had made up his mind to do a fair bit of cleaning out, as he saw it. But still he was bubbly, always joining in the banter of the dressing room, a vivid contrast with the much quieter style of both Matt Busby and Frank O'Farrell. As it turned out I wasn't going to be spending too much time with him.

Here Denis is holding forth, probably taking the mickey, setting me up for a joke. That's what Denis was like: quick-witted, absolutely wicked, brilliant company.

CHAPTER 13

BACK IN SKY BLUE

ABOVE: I hadn't planned to leave Manchester United, having agreed with Tommy Docherty that I could announce my retirement at my testimonial match in the autumn of 1973. But that summer I was in an Aberdeen pub when I saw on the television that I had been given a free transfer. I was stunned, but quickly enough I was offered a contract with Manchester City, which was highly convenient for me as I had four children and another on the way, so I wasn't keen to move house.

For the second time I was welcomed to Maine Road by Ken Barnes, now the coach, and I settled in quickly. I knew Ken, manager Johnny Hart and most of the players very well and, those being more tranquil times, there was no animosity about switching allegiances of the sort experienced by Carlos Tevez in 2009.

I was not at my physical peak but felt okay and was happy to join this City line-up for the new season. Left to right, back row: Tony Book, Colin Bell, Ron Healey, Joe Corrigan, Tommy Booth, Mike Doyle. Middle row: Ken Barnes (coach),

Mike Summerbee, myself, Rodney Marsh, Colin Barrett, Alan Oakes, Glyn Pardoe, Johnny Hart (manager). Front row: Francis Lee, Tony Whelan, Derek Jeffries, Frank Carrodus, Tony Towers, Willie Donachie.

KEN BARNES:

On my recommendation, City manager Johnny Hart brought Denis Law back to Maine Road. I knew Denis was getting on a bit, but I also knew what he had left to give. He'd had his problems with injury and most of his career was behind him. He wasn't the player he had been, but make no mistake – Denis Law was top quality, and even three-quarters of the old Denis was well worth having. I was pleased to see him back with that old swagger. He knew it was his swansong, but it was great to see him enjoy that swansong in a City shirt.

ABOVE: My much-operated-upon right knee wasn't in perfect nick; I suffered a few twinges, but still it was strong enough to propel me into the air above the likes of Tommy Smith (left) and Ian Callaghan of Liverpool. Ian was a vastly underrated footballer, a winger who could get the ball over and score a few goals, too, rather like United's John Connelly. Later he excelled as a central midfielder, but I had picked up far too many knocks to attempt a similar conversion. It was too late for me, and probably Smithy gave me one or two extra thumps during this 1-1 draw at Maine Road in April 1974 just to make sure.

TOMMY SMITH:

You might say I was known as a physical player and I must admit Denis bounced off me a time or two, but I don't believe I advanced his retirement date materially. I used to chat to opponents to put them off, maybe threatening to break their backs if they beat me – I once handed Jimmy Greaves the menu from the local hospital as we ran on to the pitch – but it was all a laugh really. Okay, maybe there was just the hint of a warning! But Denis was a mate, and he was brave as well as being one of the top players in the world. It was a man's game then, whereas now it's a fiddler's game, with players rolling on the deck for nothing at all.

ABOVE: Airborne again, this time in the 1974 League Cup final against Wolves at Wembley. We lost 2-1, which wasn't bad really when you consider that our entire forward line – Summerbee, Bell, Lee, Law and Marsh – were struggling for fitness. If the game had been a week later we'd have had a far better chance, but we didn't have a big squad and had to make the best of it. This was my last appearance at Wembley, and 'appearance' is the right word because I really don't recall competing. I'm getting in a header on goal here, but that would have been an exception. I had a truly awful game and it was extremely frustrating to be making my last appearance at the stadium without being able to do myself justice.

ABOVE: No, I didn't get a crafty transfer to Wolves before the game, although I couldn't argue if you said I was their best player! I had swapped shirts with a member of the opposition – I don't recall who – after the final whistle and although I'm having a laugh with my friend Derek Dougan, the Wolves hero and Northern Ireland international, I'm merely putting on a brave face. I can assure you I wasn't the slightest bit happy with life at that moment. Clearly the best team on the day had won, but I felt bad that our fans had no idea of our state of unfitness. They could only scratch their heads and wonder why we had played like drains.

ABOVE: This picture has to be in the book, but for me it evokes the most painful memory of my career. My backheeled goal against Manchester United at Old Trafford in April 1974 did not send my old club down to the Second Division, but it was hugely symbolic in confirming their fate and it gave me no pleasure whatsoever.

In fact, the goal was a complete fluke. The ball came across to me from Francis Lee and I flicked my foot at it almost in a random way. I didn't even know where the posts were, but somehow it wrong-footed keeper Alex Stepney and crept across the line.

It was the first time I'd ever scored a goal that made me feel sad. It wasn't nice to go back to Old Trafford, where I had played for more than a decade, known so many wonderful times and made so many friends, and then, as it were, put the final nail in their coffin.

There were various ironies that rubbed in the anguish. Steppers is a good pal of mine; Jim Holton, the United defender who was marking me, was a Scotland team-mate; and as a United player I had won the penalty which had helped to condemn City to relegation in 1963. To borrow a phrase of Sir Alex Ferguson's: football, bloody hell!

ALEX STEPNEY:

It had come as a devastating shock to the United players when Denis left so unexpectedly, because we heard he had been promised another contract. But then for him to score this goal was utterly demoralising, both for us and for him.

He's a good friend and I felt deeply for him. We knew we were going down anyway, but to see him turn away with his head lowered after the ball crept over the line was completely awful.

ABOVE: It's pretty unusual to be consoled after scoring a goal, but I was grateful to Mike Summerbee for his sympathetic attitude after my infamous backheel at Old Trafford. He was City through and through, had been a fierce rival of United for years and always possessed a wicked sense of humour, so those who didn't know him well might have expected him to take the mick. But he and I had been friends for a long time, he was a close pal of Bestie, and he sensed this wasn't the moment to be crowing or pulling my leg.

A couple of the City lads might have celebrated – it would be hard to imagine Mike Doyle keeping a straight face in these circumstances – but most of them recognised this was a difficult moment for me and reacted with genuine sensitivity.

And, after all, football clubs and their fans need their local rivals to be in the same division. Without local derbies the game would not be nearly so enjoyable.

MIKE SUMMERBEE:

Denis has always been a hero to me and that has never changed. He is a deeply emotional person and I knew how much he loved United. He didn't want to say goodbye to them by scoring the goal that confirmed their relegation, and I felt for him. At that moment, he needed an arm around his shoulder and I was glad to be there for him.

ABOVE: I was always telling Mike Summerbee he should do something to improve his looks, but this is ridiculous! It would seem he's attempting an impression of the hunchback Quasimodo, but he's put the ball up the wrong side of his shirt. Mind you, it wasn't unusual for Mike to stick the ball in the wrong place.

He was, and remains, a huge extrovert, but that didn't mean that he failed to take the game seriously. He was a quick and skilful outside-right, but also very, very hard. Usually you would hear about wingers not wanting to face tough-nut full-backs, but in Mike's case it was the other way round.

Here I'm pointing the ugly duckling in the direction of the camera, while Francis Lee (next to me) and Rodney Marsh are much amused. We always managed to have a laugh in training. Footballers are richer now, but I wonder if they have as much fun.

MIKE SUMMERBEE:

This was just a spontaneous bit of fun. Denis always had a smile on his face, he would light up any room with his cracking sense of humour, and he loved the banter of footballers. The bulge at the back is my attempt to imitate Quasimodo, and certainly not a show of disrespect for anyone with a disability, as was once suggested. As for the bulge at the front, I guess I had put on a bit of weight . . .

ABOVE: Scotland's twin strikers? Not quite, although Rod Stewart loves his football and is a decent player, what you might call a dashing attacker and a lovely passer of the ball. He knows the game thoroughly, too, and is so enthusiastic that often he has chartered a plane to take him from London to Hampden Park for an international. He's got a full-sized pitch in his back garden, which is manicured as beautifully as Wembley used to be, and he uses it for charity matches.

Here I'm presenting him with a gold disc for his album *Play It Again, Rod* in 1973. He used to take the mick out of me for liking Sinatra, but then many years later he actually put out an album of crooner music! Rod's got a fabulous voice, certainly, but that didn't sound right to me. I've got to hand it to him, though, he's looked after himself and nearly four decades later he's in better nick than ever.

ROD STEWART:

The first time I met Denis he immediately mocked me for the size of my hooter. I quickly replied with rapier wit: 'That's hardly a little button in the middle of your face, mate.' And we've been best friends ever since. Denis was one of the most stylish players to grace the beautiful game, but more importantly he's one hell of a good bloke. Your round, Denis!

CHAPTER 14

LAST SWING OF THE CLAYMORE

LEFT: After three years of injury and frustration, in the spring of 1972 I was asked to pull on a Scotland shirt again, and the sense of privilege was just as sharp and meaningful as it had been nearly a decade and a half earlier when I had been a snotty-nosed rookie at Huddersfield. That deep, rich shade of blue, contrasting so vividly with the red lion rampant on the crest, sums up for me all the pride and the passion evoked by playing for my country. It will never cease to move me.

OPPOSITE: Though I was into my thirties when I received my international recall, and some of my joints creaked like the hinges of a rusty door, I could still raise a bit of a gallop. Here, at Hampden Park in May 1972, I've got Northern Ireland's posts in my sights and that afternoon I managed to score my 30th and last goal for Scotland. It was a record at the time, but it's since been equalled by Kenny Dalglish. I'm sure there's nothing either of us would like better than to see a new Scottish sharp-shooter pass our mark, but the fortunes of our national team have declined dramatically since our days, so it would be fair to say we're not exactly holding our breath.

ABOVE: Foiled again. Clearly I'm exasperated, either with myself for missing a sitter or with a team-mate whose final ball didn't meet my requirements. Meanwhile, Northern Ireland keeper Pat Jennings is calling for the ball to take a goal-kick. It's funny, but his hands look relatively normal here, yet when I've been close to him on the pitch they've always reminded me of buckets. He could pick up a football with one hand as if it were a tennis ball, and he had an irritating knack of plucking a cross from the sky just when I thought I was going to nod it into his net. Pat was a remarkable keeper, undoubtedly one of the best ever, and I have relished our rivalry as much as I still treasure our friendship.

I'm looking unfeasibly good-humoured here, considering I've got my arm round Alan Ball, the man who has just scored the only goal of the game for England against Scotland at Hampden Park in May 1972. But despite his excitable part in my sending-off at Blackpool back in the mists of time, it was impossible to remain at odds with such an enthusiastic little character – and he was little, wasn't he? Barely up to my shoulder and I'm no giant. But what a player he was; certainly he was one of the great England footballers of his generation, and one who made a colossal difference to the team that, I'm told, picked up some trophy or another in 1966!

Alan had a fantastic motor as well as remarkable skill and I'm surprised that Manchester United never really went after him. He would have been a magnificent addition to Frank O'Farrell's team in the early 1970s, and he was just the sort to build a side around for the rest of the decade.

ABOVE: Tommy Docherty has always had the knack of making people laugh, and here he's got Bobby Moncur chuckling and me guffawing at the Scotland team hotel in 1972, not too long before he took over at Old Trafford. I think he did really well as our national manager, making people believe in themselves, but for Scottish fans it was hard to lose a successful boss to a club.

The Doc was still looking great in his eighties, but actually he looked 70-odd when he was 40 so he's never changed a great deal. I don't bear any ill will now over my United exit. It wasn't nice at the time and I didn't get what he promised me, but time has healed things, and it is fair to say I was past my best anyway.

Bobby Moncur, who went on to become a transatlantic yachtsman after retiring from football, is looking dapper as always. He's a good lad with a tag he's increasingly desperate to lose. I know he feels the honour of being the last Newcastle skipper to lift a major trophy, the Fairs Cup in 1969, but he'd love nothing better than to see someone else take on the mantle.

ABOVE: Going face to face, or maybe that should be toe to hand, with Gordon Banks in my last international against England, at Hampden Park in May 1972. The ball's on the end of my foot as I stretch but it's not under control, far from it. And although I'd like to say my pointing finger is telling Gordon it's headed for his top corner, that's just wishful thinking because we lost 1-0.

England were very fortunate at the time to have three or four top keepers from whom to choose, but there's no question that Gordon is the best I've ever seen. A few come close – the likes of Lev Yashin, Pat Jennings and Peter Schmeichel, and Peter Shilton and Ray Clemence were no mugs, either – but Banksie was in a class all of his own.

Looking at the crowd, as I always like to do, I can again spy plenty of girls. Now they couldn't have turned up to watch George Best on this occasion, so maybe I *was* a sex symbol after all . . .

GORDON BANKS:

When I faced Denis he nearly always scored a goal, so I was delighted to come out on the right side for once, especially in front of 120,000 fans, most of whom were roaring on the Scots. He was a truly great player and is a smashing guy. But sex symbol? Well, I suppose his shorts were very short ...

ABOVE: I'm looking on in sheer admiration as Joe Jordan flies through the air to score the goal that beat Czechoslovakia, one of the best sides in Europe, at Hampden Park in September 1973, thus taking Scotland to the World Cup finals in Germany the following summer. We hadn't qualified since 1958, a gap of 16 years, which is longer than most careers. I believe we were good enough to get there in both 1962 and 1966 but we were unlucky both times. Now I had the chance to end my international days on a high. After leaving United in such troubled circumstances, and suffering more injuries – this was my first game for Scotland for 15 months – I considered myself a very fortunate fellow.

I think I had a decent game for new boss Willie Ormond, while Joe Jordan was absolutely immense. He was enough to scare the Czechs to death, hurling himself at them fearlessly, snarling through that big gap in his fangs like some better-looking version of Nobby Stiles. Joe didn't score that many goals because he was primarily a target man, although he was a joy to play alongside because he battled for everything. But this header was a real belter and the Czech keeper didn't have a hope of keeping it out.

ABOVE: By the look of my celebration, you would think I'd scored the goal myself. Well, let me tell you that I was just as overjoyed as if it had been me who had buried that beautiful cross from Willie Morgan. This was one of the happiest moments of my professional life and if anyone thought I was going to content myself with a sober nod before strolling back to the centre circle in an orderly fashion, then they didn't know me at all.

ABOVE: That head of red curls I'm snuggling up to belongs to Billy Bremner, our wee firecracker of a skipper, and this victory meant everything to him. He was a world-class performer and this was the first time he had reached the biggest stage of all. Maybe our team wasn't quite on a par with the two that had missed out so agonisingly in the 1960s, but still it was an excellent one and we believed we were equipped to give a decent account of ourselves at the ultimate level. Above all, we had given something back to the fans who had been suffering dismal disappointment for so, so long.

ABOVE: This is how Scotland lined up in Dortmund for my first match in a World Cup finals tournament and the last of my international career. We were facing Zaire, about whom we knew virtually nothing, and when we went 2-0 up probably we rowed back a bit, playing safe and making absolutely sure we won. In the end that proved our downfall. Though we remained unbeaten after draws with Brazil and Yugoslavia in which I didn't play, we went out on goal difference. The mighty South Americans were only one goal better off than Scotland – enough for them, agonising for us.

Looking at this group now, I feel so sad because of Big Jim Holton (standing second from left), at the time a colossal presence in the rearguards of both Manchester United and his country. He was the sort of comrade you'd want beside you on any battlefield, and it was so tragic that he died in his early forties. On the left of the front row is Kenny Dalglish, as fine a player as Scotland has ever known, and that's saying something. I'd love it if we could find another Dalglish, but I think we'd be very fortunate.

Left to right, back row: David Harvey, Jim Holton, Joe Jordan, Danny McGrain, John Blackley. Front row: Kenny Dalglish, Sandy Jardine, Peter Lorimer, Billy Bremner, David Hay and myself.

DANNY McGRAIN:

When I began to play for Scotland in 1973, I didn't know what to expect from Denis Law. To be honest, I was petrified about meeting such an icon of the world game. I half expected that when he walked through the door he would be surrounded by white mist, like some celestial being. But he turned out to be such a nice, softly spoken guy, invariably with a cup of tea in his hand, and that taught all the youngsters in the squad a lesson about how to behave. I've never heard anyone say a bad thing about Denis, either as a player or a person, and I'm proud to know him.

OPPOSITE: I'm a sucker for shots of me in the Scotland kit. Those distinctive colours get me every time. This portrait was taken by Manchester-based Harry Goodwin, one of the finest snappers of the last half a century or so, a lively veteran who was still taking terrific pictures in his eighties.

ABOVE: I played table tennis so much in my youth club days that I couldn't help being fairly good at it, but somehow I never got the hang of playing doubles. My problem, as wee Jimmy Johnstone discovered during this game when we were in Germany for the 1974 World Cup finals, was that I wanted to hit every ball myself. Here he thinks he's about to play a shot, but I'm poised to push him out of the way.

Jimmy was an unforgettable character, a lovely, lovely guy. Just look at the happiness on his face; it makes me weep to think he's gone. People outside the game might not realise that he was a talented singer who could handle Sinatra-type crooning or the brand of lively and soulful rock music purveyed by our mate Rod Stewart.

We all know he was an incredible footballer, but he was a glorious all-round sportsman, too. He was particularly excellent at rowing, I believe. Had he been at Oxford or Cambridge he'd have been a cert for the Boat Race, though his build and his proven navigational skills suggested he'd have been in his element as a cox.

My international farewell came against Zaire in Dortmund in June 1974, nearly 16 years on from my debut against Wales as a very green and excited teenager.

LEFT: It was very hot and I needed one or two breathers, but I remained as eager for the fray as ever. You see, once you have the taste for top-level competition you want it again and again, but I knew in my heart my time was up.

OPPOSITE: Taking a tumble against the Leopards, who were making the most of their first World Cup finals. I threw myself into things as passionately as ever and my poor old wrist took a bit of a battering as I attempted to break my fall. Luckily the grass was quite long – either that or my hand has disappeared down a hole.

TOP: Proof that I still had a bit of spring in the old pins and I managed to go close a couple of times. But not close enough . . .

CHAPTER 15

A LONG TIME RETIRED

ABOVE: I hope nobody is cynical enough to suggest this picture was posed. There I was, a typically good-humoured Scotsman, gambolling along Regent Street in my kilt, merrily contemplating my country's prospects in the forthcoming World Cup in Argentina, when a cameraman happened to pop round the corner. It was nice of the London traffic to stop so I could cross the road outside the BBC offices. I can only surmise the motorists were enchanted by my spontaneous rendition of 'Don't Cry For Me, Argentina'!

You want the truth? Okay, I was plugging the Beeb's coverage of the tournament, in which I would play a part. Argentina was an exciting place to go, having just undergone a political coup, and I must admit I was a bit anxious – especially as I was travelling under the banner of the BBC, which had criticised the South Americans' government so roundly. As it turned out, we were closely watched and it was quite frightening. I can assure you that behind all this frivolity were serious apprehensions. And no, I didn't leave home in my kilt that morning. Di would have had me locked up.

ABOVE: I thoroughly enjoyed life as a broadcaster, working for the BBC between 1978 and 1990. I was a summariser, and as I didn't know a lot about some of the international teams, I had to do my homework. It was a pleasure to accompany some great commentators, the likes of Peter Jones, Alan Parry and Bryon Butler, all excellent professionals. They were smashing characters and a huge help to me. I like to think I brought something to the table, too, not least the fact that I had a certain amount of access to reach players and managers for interviews, because I had been in the game. It was all about teamwork, just like football. Still, I didn't realise how hard radio could be until I did it. Did I understand all the equipment? Did I hell!

RIGHT: I've had a few early baths in my time, but usually I took my clothes off first! Here I was in the Anfield dressing room, working on my notes ahead of a commentary, and I was consigned to the bath because there weren't enough seats. Actually it was a nice, quiet spot where I could relax, at least until I was spotted by a photographer. Still, they gave me a cup of tea – I could always count on top treatment at Anfield . . .

ABOVE: People tell me how Nat Lofthouse (left) was so brilliant in the air, but I'm outjumping him easily here, and I'm managing to tower above Tom Finney, too, even if I am getting a lift by leaning on their shoulders. Of course, I should point out that these two great gentlemen of English football were in their sixties at the time, and if they'd been in their pomp no doubt they'd have left me standing. Considering their colossal achievements in the game, it was a huge honour for me just to be in the same picture. They are absolute icons and were friendly, modest men, too. Here we were promoting a campaign to improve youngsters' football skills, and nobody could wish for better role models than Nat and Tom.

ABOVE: I was on my way to audition as the new Dr Who when I dropped in at Wembley for the 1991 League Cup final, in which Manchester United lost to Sheffield Wednesday. That's my story and I'm sticking to it. Actually, I did love that coat, which kept me warm in many a draughty press box down the years. Believe it or not, I bought it in Marbella in the middle of summer, when the temperature was touching the nineties. I always had an eye for a bargain.

ABOVE: When I was a skinny lad, the son of a fisherman, kicking a ball against a wall in Printfield Terrace, Aberdeen, I never dreamt that the game would take me on to the roof of BBC headquarters in London along with some of the most famous sportsmen and women in the land. But that's where I found myself when the *Radio Times* needed a photograph of their sports broadcasters all together, although I'm not sure what Terry Wogan (left) is doing there.

The rest of us, left to right, are swimmer Anita Lonsbrough, myself – complete with a barnet that was perfect for radio! – athlete Mary Peters, boxer Henry Cooper, tennis player Christine Truman, jockey John Oaksey and cricketer Tony Lewis, clutching a daffodil to prove he's Welsh.

They were a terrific bunch of people and it was exciting to work with them. Broadcasting was just what I needed at the end of my football career. I never entertained the idea of coaching or management, although it might be different today, given the money that's in the game now. I could work for a year, then get the sack and retire on the proceeds.

OPPOSITE: The things some people will do for publicity. Now, the World Cup I was plugging – where could it possibly have been? And where were the other two amigos? I never felt the merest shred of shame when I was doing this type of work, and I must say that no sombrero had been worn so stylishly since Bestie came back from Lisbon after United thrashed Benfica in 1966. His life was never the same after that. Mine might have changed after this – I might have been put in prison.

ABOVE: Meet my secretary. She was a hard worker with an enquiring mind, though I must admit she was a wee bit high-maintenance if we ever wandered near a sweet shop. This was my daughter Little Di – as distinct from my wife, Big Di – helping me to get a few notes together for a broadcast. She was about five at the time and now it strikes me that she was the spitting image of my granddaughter Emilia, Andrew's little girl. I'm demonstrating how I typed with only two fingers, which was easily quick enough for my brain.

ABOVE: Bryan Robson goes down as one of the greatest names in Manchester United history and it was a privilege for me to make this presentation to him before his final game for the club, at home to Coventry in May 1994. He was unfortunate not to peak when the team was at its best, but he did enough to collect a title medal in each of his last two seasons. On this occasion, the prize had already been won, which was just as well as the game finished 0-0.

ABOVE: I had known Sir Matt Busby throughout my foot-balling life, right back to my time as a Scotland Schoolboy, and I thoroughly enjoyed the different phase of our relationship after I had laid aside my boots. Now we were no longer player and manager, but a couple of friends who happened to hail from the same country and with plenty in common.

In the early 1990s, during his spell as club president and towards the end of his life, I loved to call on him in the little office United still provided for him at Old Trafford, a place that enabled him still to feel part of the club that he had created in its modern form. We would sit and drink a cup of tea while chewing the fat about anything and everything.

I know he felt warmed by the achievements of another fellow Scot, Alex Ferguson. They had the same feelings towards the game and felt the same obligation to entertain the people who paid to watch it, but there were contrasts between them. You would never see Matt jumping up and down when United scored a goal, a satisfied nod of the head was the most emotion he'd show. I suppose anybody who smokes a pipe tends to be a bit calmer.

ABOVE: Ouch! Nobby Stiles puts the squeeze on me at a party to celebrate the 30th anniversary of Manchester United's first European Cup triumph. I have all the time in the world for Nobby, a magnificent footballer for club and country and one of the most down-to-earth characters you could ever hope to find.

When we all get back together he's always the same, definitely one of the grumpy brigade, just like me and most of the others as we tear our hair about modern players and some of their exploits. Nobby's always wearing his Eric Morecambe glasses, and often he used to act like Eric, too. He was renowned for being clumsy, he was always bumping into something, such as the time he had a minor accident in his car. He and the other motorist involved bent down to examine the damage and they knocked their heads together. It could only happen to Nobby.

NOBBY STILES:

I'm not putting the squeeze on Denis. I wouldn't dare! He's just winding up the photographer by pretending he's in agony. Mind, we might have caused each other a bit of pain when England played Scotland. He was always good for a laugh and a joke, but when he was representing his country there wasn't a more serious man on the planet.

OPPOSITE: Little Boys Blue. The uniforms my old United mate David Sadler and I wore when we were part of the team that carried the Commonwealth Games baton around Manchester in 2002 were certainly a bit of an eyeful, but it was worth it for the honour. Saddy looks better now, don't you think?

DAVID SADLER:

As you can see from my waistline, although not from Denis's, many years have passed since our playing days. The organisers wanted two former United players, one to ferry the baton from Stretford to Old Trafford, which Denis did, and the other to jog around the stadium before passing it on, which fell to me. When we'd done our bits we popped into Old Trafford for a cuppa, although really I think we deserved something stronger.

Later I wore the shirt at a croquet afternoon with a few friends. I got some funny looks – can't think why . . .

ABOVE: Another reunion of the '68-ers, this time in Belfast in 1999. We were a close-knit team and will always share something that nobody else can. The old relationship is always intact when we get back together and it's fair to say that we always have a grand time. The clock behind the bar is saying it's three o'clock, and I guess that must be in the afternoon because we're all standing.

Left to right are John Aston, Dave Sadler, Bobby Charlton, myself, the landlord, Bill Foulkes, Nobby Stiles, Tony Dunne, Paddy Crerand, Harry Gregg, Brian Kidd and Alex Stepney. Shay Brennan and George Best were still with us at this point, but for some reason they were missing from the picture.

ABOVE: This is a happy shot of three old muckers, cuddling for the camera in 1995. If anybody'd told me 40 years ago that one day there'd be a statue of Bobby, Bestie and myself outside Old Trafford, I'd have thought they were bonkers. As the decades passed the three of us grew closer than ever before. Somehow the age gap doesn't matter so much when you're older because differences in outlook seem to diminish. Bobby's looking especially cheerful here – or maybe he's got wind!

ABOVE: What am I doing with my little finger? Proving that I'm posh – it's all a matter of breeding, you know. Nobby, Paddy and Bobby wouldn't have understood.

We were getting our feet cast in plaster for a proposed Walk of Fame at Old Trafford in 2000. They were hoping to sell imprints, too, but not surprisingly the venture never took off. Who wants a plaque of somebody's feet in their house, complete with bunions? It was a very odd concept, but at least it gave us all a laugh. Of course, Paddy had peculiar feet anyway, pointing inwards like a pigeon's.

And yes, of course that's how I drink my tea at home. Class will out!

PADDY CRERAND:

Denis was always mad for tea. He was a chain drinker of the stuff. When he walked into your house he didn't ask you to make tea, he'd go straight to the kitchen and put the kettle on himself. I'm not so sure about his poshness, though . . .

I started the new millennium by going down with prostate cancer, and after I was lucky enough to recover I got involved in the Man Alive campaign, which aims to convince people that they can be positive and survive the condition, provided that they face it. The fact is that too many people brush aside their symptoms and put off seeing the doctor. If any man feels that something is not quite right, then he should take medical advice. A five-minute chat will tell them either that they can forget about it, or that they might need an investigation to sort it out.

You're not messing the doctor about, and you could be saving your life. I'm a good example. Stupidly, I put it off for ages, but then my wife Di made me go. Now I'm the living proof that I did the right thing in the end.

I hope these pictures, taken to publicise the campaign, did some good by increasing awareness. I'm looking pretty chirpy in three of the shots, while let's just say the other one caught me in an unguarded moment. If that's what I look like when I'm healthy, clearly you wouldn't want to see me looking ill.

ABOVE: Have I been hiding my academic light under a bushel? Not exactly, but I was delighted to accept honorary degrees from the universities of St Andrews (left) and Aberdeen. I can only imagine that St Andrews was struggling for recipients, but I feel genuinely humble that they chose me, and I was delighted when somebody threw a ball at my feet. It was better to try a bit of keepy-uppy than having to make a speech.

It was tremendous to get the call from my home city, too, especially as I ended up with such a nice hat into the bargain. The award meant so much to me and my family – I've lost two brothers, but I've still got two sisters and a brother living in Aberdeen.

Di seems amazed by the headgear and I'm not surprised. It makes me look like one of the ancient wizards in *Harry Potter*. Of course, the gowns were special, but I must admit I was most made up about that hat. Actually, I'm probably daft to mention that because I nicked it, right enough. I hope they don't come after it.

ABOVE: An occasion both happy and poignant in November 2005. Happy, because it gave Bobby and me the opportunity to pay tribute to the incomparable talent of George Best, and to remember him with joy in our hearts. Poignant, because it reminded us that only recently Bestie had been taken away from us.

Somehow his European Footballer of the Year trophy, which he won in 1968, had been mislaid, so the magazine *France Football*, which launched the award half a century earlier, asked the two of us – as fellow recipients and former United team-mates – to receive this modern version of the Ballon D'Or on behalf of his family. This one is much bigger than the original, and is the size the winners get now. The honour, though, remains the same.

BELOW: Who's the skinhead having a giggle with England World Cup winner Roger Hunt and me at Old Trafford in October 2006, when United were playing Liverpool and a host of old players had gathered to celebrate the 50th anniversary of Bobby Charlton's first-team debut? One theory is that it's Uncle Fester, and it does look like him from the back. Or from the front, actually. But closer examination shows it to be Wilf McGuinness, the one-time United player and manager who now works for the club in corporate hospitality. As for Roger, he was always a good lad with a smashing sense of humour. Thinking back to 1966, though, it's a shame about his eyesight.

WILF McGUINNESS:

Roger likes a laugh – and I think Denis must have told him the wages he used to be on at Old Trafford.

ROGER HUNT:

Denis seems very happy here – obviously he hasn't been told there is no fee involved!

ABOVE: When Old Trafford hosted the European Cup final between AC Milan and Juventus in May 2003, the game turned out to be a goalless bore, eventually settled in Milan's favour by penalties – or so I'm told by those who managed to stay awake – but the socialising before and after the football was something else.

The biggest magnet for me was the chance to catch up again with my boyhood idol, Alfredo di Stefano (centre). Real Madrid were the holders, so he was there to hand in the trophy, and is sharing a laugh here with Bobby Charlton, Paddy Crerand and myself. The Great Man was looking very well, sporting the same hairstyle he had when he was playing, and we reminisced at length about the time we were team-mates for the Rest of the World against England way back in 1963. Whenever people argue about who was the greatest footballer of all time, the two names that invariably crop up are Pelé and Maradona. Well, for me, you can add Alfredo's moniker to that select list, and he might just get my vote. I've never seen anybody make the game look easier, and he's a lovely person, too.

LEFT: No matter how long the gap between get-togethers, the old chemistry between Bestie and myself never went flat. There was always a thread between us that stretched unbroken back to the days when we had travelled the world with Manchester United, and that was apparent in Castlereagh, Northern Ireland, on this evening in April 2002 when he was being given the freedom of the borough. He was looking pretty good at the time and was on great form. That's probably his notes for his speech that he's clutching behind my back, and he would have been worth listening to because he was both very intelligent and, usually, extremely funny.

BELOW: I'm as pleased as punch to be opening the Scottish Football Hall of Fame at Hampden Park in November 2004. My overriding emotion is one of delighted amazement that I should find my own name on a list of so many all-time greats. Either that or I'm launching a career as a stand-up comedian, a proposition not to be contemplated, as all my pals would no doubt tell you!

ABOVE: I always relished wearing United's No 10, and when the club announced in the summer of 2007 that it was passing to Wayne Rooney, I was delighted to do the honours. I can't really put my finger on my attraction to that particular shirt, but I was just comfortable with it. I started as an old-fashioned up-and-down inside-forward, usually being allocated No 8 for both Huddersfield and Manchester City, but when I came to Old Trafford Albert Quixall was in possession of that so I was given the inside-left's No 10, and it stuck, even when I was up front as an out-and-out striker.

I couldn't have wished for a more accomplished successor, football-wise, than Wayne. If he stays at Old Trafford and remains largely injury-free then I'd expect him to drive a cart and horses through all United's scoring records. Of course, he'll have to survive untold pressure both on and off the pitch, as we've seen recently, but I wish him well. When I handed over the shirt at Carrington, he seemed a very quiet lad, but then, what do I know?

WAYNE ROONEY:

This was a truly magical moment for me. When Ruud van Nistelrooy left the club his No 10 shirt became available, and I said I'd like to take it on. But by that time they'd sold shirts with my No 8 on for the coming season so they said I would have to wait a year. Eventually, when I returned from my next summer break, I was overwhelmed to learn that the great Denis Law was going to present me with the No 10 shirt. It was an unbelievable honour because he was such an Old Trafford legend, a man who had scored so many goals for Manchester United. I'd watched him on DVDs and knew he was a brilliant centre-forward who was so brave in the box and who scored goals of every type, including loads of headers even though he was not the tallest of men. I'll treasure the memory of receiving the No 10 from Denis as long as I live.

ABOVE: How was your steak, sir? Well, I think talented newcomers in any field deserve loads of encouragement and I can thoroughly recommend this promising young chef, who came up with a delicious meal for me as part of the MUTV cookery progamme, *Red Devils' Kitchen*. There was service with a smile, too, but you might wonder why Sir Alex Ferguson, the gastronomic maestro in question, was kitted out with blue gloves. In fact, he was sharpening a knife, but pulled it towards himself instead of pushing it away as he should have done, and he cut his finger so badly that he needed the gloves to keep his blood out of my food. To be fair, he deserved a tip but I didn't leave one because the bill never arrived. So what's my final word on the Ferguson cuisine? Terrific, but keep him away from the cutlery!

SIR ALEX FERGUSON:

I'd like to say that I cut myself because I was so terrified that Denis wouldn't like my culinary fare. After all, people who remember him as a player might think that he's a frightening man away from the pitch, too. In fact, he's a pussycat and a lovely human being.

ABOVE: It's always nice to get your hands on some silverware, even if you've done nothing to earn it. This was at Eastlands in the spring of 2008 and the bauble I'm clutching is the UEFA Cup. I was due to help Michel Platini with the presentations after the game between Rangers and Zenit St Petersburg, in which the Russians triumphed deservedly thanks to a couple of late goals. At this point, I think I'm looking for a convenient place to put the cup down. It was so incredibly heavy, if I'd been the winning captain I doubt if I could have lifted it above my head.

I enjoyed the occasion, which was sadly marred by some terrible violence afterwards. I didn't know anything about it at the time, but the pictures on television were horrific, with some of the policemen being lucky to escape with their lives. It was all very sad, and a powerful argument in favour of those who don't want to resume regular meetings between England and Scotland.

ABOVE: 'Come on Dad, you're in the wrong place!' Being ordered around by my daughter Di at Wembley in May 2007, when United played Chelsea in the first FA Cup final at the new stadium. She was working as United's player liaison officer at the time and it looks to me as if she was throwing her weight about. I'm trying to remind her that I retired a long time ago so I'm not under her jurisdiction, but she's having none of it!

It was my first visit to the new ground and I was astounded by the awful state of the pitch, which was ridiculous given the vast sums of money spent on the project. As for the game, it was deadly dull and drove me to sleep. The only goal, scored by Didier Drogba, didn't come until near the end and it failed to wake me up.

OPPOSITE: Here's the wisest and wittiest man in football – and the fella in the red cap knew a bit about the game, too! Of course, I'm joking, because John Doherty, as well as being one of my dearest friends, was the fount of all football knowledge as far as I was concerned. He was one of the original Busby Babes, a creative inside-forward who helped to win the league title in 1955-56, only to be invalided out of the game by a terrible knee injury.

John wrote one of the best football books there will ever be, *The Insider's Guide to Manchester United*, in which he ran the rule over every player since the war. You might call it forthright – at least, that's one way of putting it. He wasn't a man given to holding back, except in one or two instances which might have landed him in court. But while his comments could be a wee bit acerbic, shall we say, he never criticised for the sake of it, only when it was deserved.

Another of his major achievements was as leading light of the Association of Former Manchester United Players, which has raised huge sums for charities down the years. He was a fine golfer, too, invariably hitting the ball straight down the middle of the fairway. He wasn't the fittest so he didn't get the distance, but his hand–eye co-ordination was exceptional and there weren't many who would beat him off a handicap.

JD was a lovely, warm, loyal, acutely intelligent, occasionally fierce, very funny man, and I have missed him so much since his death in 2007.

JOHN DOHERTY:

Denis is a smashing fellow, such a nice man, so very different from that spiky persona on the field. He's an exceptionally private person, except in the company of those who know him well, and then he's the wickedest mickey-taker you could imagine. If you're a friend, you've got a chance with Denis. Otherwise forget it.

TOP: I'm showing off here, attempting to pass the ball between the legs of JD's grandson, James, while doing a bit of publicity for one of the most worthwhile causes I know. The girl in the picture is Tracy, JD's daughter, who recovered from breast cancer and then launched Worth A Whistle, a campaign to fight the disease. In front of the bushes in the garden of the Christie Hospital, no doubt having a go at my technique on the ball, is John himself, while the two professionals are Tracy's oncologist Alan Stewart and the superintendent radiographer Julia Barker.

ABOVE: Bidding farewell to something that has played an emotional part in your life is always poignant, and certainly that was the case for me when Manchester United made the decision to demolish the Stretford End in the summer of 1992. Gazing up from the pitch, I didn't really see the empty, litter-strewn terracing. In my mind was that rolling, heaving bank of intensely excited humanity that towered above the players throughout my United career.

How did it feel to run out in front of the Stretford End? It was a huge bonus to me, just like the Hampden Roar, and it must have been terrifying for visiting players who weren't used to such a din. What was it like to be known as The King? Well, it was a tremendous honour, but a wee bit embarrassing, too. I really didn't want my earlier book to be called *The King*, but my publisher insisted. Looking back, I wish I'd been stronger on that.

Regarding the demolition, of course I understand concerns following horrific accidents in other grounds, but sometimes I feel the health-and-safety argument goes a bit over the top.

ABOVE: Now listen to me, son, this is how you do it! Only kidding, of course, because Cristiano Ronaldo doesn't need advice from me or anybody else. You might say he's a fairly confident boy, which was evident when I met him on the pitch at Old Trafford in December 2008 to mark his recent coronation as European Footballer of the Year. Bobby Charlton and I were there, as previous holders of the award, and we both had to look up to the young man, because he's much taller than I had imagined from merely watching him play. Obviously, he's one of the best footballers in the world, and I was sad to see him leave United only a few months later.

CLIFF BUTLER:

When I was a United-daft youngster, Denis Law was my hero. He played a huge part in my childhood and beyond. There was just something about him and the way he played the game. He was a bloody rascal, right in the middle of everything. You might say George was for the girls, Bobby was for the dads and Denis was for the lads.

In 1983 I was out of work, having just been made redundant after a decade with Port of Manchester Warehouses, but for six years had been United's official statistician, then an unpaid position.

One day I was in the club office when Denis walked in and we started chatting. It turned out that we were both unemployed, Denis being between broadcasting jobs, and he asked me how I was managing. I admitted that things were a bit tight financially, so much so that I hadn't yet been able to buy the latest edition of the Rothmans Football Yearbook, *generally considered to be the game's statistical bible.*

The next day when I went back to the office I was told to look in a certain drawer, which I did, and found a copy of the new Rothmans. *Imagine my astonishment when I was told that Denis had left it for me. It was like Frank Sinatra bestowing his latest disc on one of his fans. It was an incredibly generous gesture and one that I'll never forget. I still have the book and it has pride of place in my library.*

People say you should never meet your hero because you'll be disappointed, but that certainly wasn't the case for me. He was my hero then and, if I'm honest, he still is and always will be.

DENIS:

Cliff was doing a very important job for the club. At that time, as is still the case, if you wanted to know anything about Manchester United or its history, he was the man to ask. I guess I felt he needed to have the right tools at his disposal. In those days there was a real family feel to the club and Cliff was both a member of that family and a very genuine lad. Mind, knowing how much he loves his books, I never told him that I'd got it second-hand . . .

CHAPTER 16

THE ONES WHO MATTER MOST

ABOVE: Halfway through my first season at Manchester United, my mind was on more than football. Di and me shortly before our wedding in December 1962. The look of love? Well, that might describe my expression, but I've got a feeling Di might be telling me off – some things never change.

ABOVE: The big day, and I must say the bride was looking radiant. And, as I said, some things never change.

RIGHT: Here's proof positive that I was a 'new man' before they even invented the term. This was when I was suspended in January 1965, so I thought I'd put some of that unexpected spare time to good use by helping to look after our first-born, Gary – or maybe my wife, Di, made the decision for me.

Look at that pram – they don't make 'em like that any more. They were proper prams, not like some of the complicated contraptions you see nowadays. It was built to last, nice and sturdy, something you could carry a sack of coal in if the need arose!

ABOVE: Though my family grew up in England all the children remain proud Scots. I wonder why! But no matter what you're thinking, I didn't make them all wear Scotland pyjamas. This was just a publicity shot before I left for the World Cup finals in 1974. Little Di is the bonny baby on Big Di's knee while the boys, in ascending order, are Iain, Robert, Andrew and Gary.

Contrary to general perceptions, they are not all football fans. For some mysterious reason, Iain followed Everton for a while but then gave it up; Robert isn't even interested in the game, he's more into technical things. But I guess it would have been strange if none of them were into football, and Andrew is a City fanatic, while Gary and Di follow United. So that's 2-1 to United with two abstentions.

OPPOSITE: Di is looking suitably impressed by my vintage headgear, though she might be advocating a minor adjustment. A more rakish angle perhaps? England players used to get a cap every time they played, but we received only one to cover each season in which we were selected.

OPPOSITE: Oooh, I hope Little Di's perch on that garden gate is more comfortable than it looks! Instead of making sure she's comfortable, the rest of us are concentrating on the camera. Her brothers, left to right, are Robert, Andrew, Gary and Iain.

ABOVE: I take it as an incredible honour to have a statue of myself at the entrance to the Stretford End, but sometimes it feels a bit spooky to look at it because it's so huge, something like 12 feet high. It's a bit big for the space really, and there was talk of moving it, but I'm told the Stretford Enders wouldn't hear of it. Alex Ferguson and the United chairman at the time, Martin Edwards, were there with Di and me for the unveiling.

ABOVE: It's embarrassing enough to have one statue of yourself, let alone two. This one is out in the open where everybody can see it, on Sir Matt Busby Way, and I'm delighted that it's not just me posing eternally for the fans' pictures, but Bobby and George are up there too. It was marvellous to have most of the family there when the covers came off. At the back, left to right, are Robert Buckley, Little Di's husband; Gary's partner Beverley and their two boys, James and Harvey; Gary; Robert; Big Di and me. At the front are Andrew's wife Marie; Little Di holding Emilia, Andrew's girl, and Andrew. Unfortunately we couldn't get the complete line-up because Iain was away at the time.

ACKNOWLEDGEMENTS

My family, for putting up with me and looking after me

Sir Alex Ferguson, for the generosity and the vivid imagination of his foreword

Also, for trying to keep a straight face while uttering their kind words: Gordon Banks, Cliff Butler, Sir Bobby Charlton, Jack Charlton, John Connelly, Paddy Crerand, Alex Dawson, Tony Dunne, Bill Foulkes, Jimmy Greaves, David Herd, Roger Hunt, Brian Kidd, Danny McGrain, Wilf McGuinness, Dave Mackay, Les Massie, Wayne Rooney, David Sadler, Ian St John, Tommy Smith, Alex Stepney, Rod Stewart, Nobby Stiles, Mike Summerbee

Finally, I'd like to pay tribute to the great men whose words have appeared posthumously: Alan Ball, Ken Barnes, George Best, Sir Matt Busby, John Doherty, Jimmy Murphy, Bill Shankly

Denis' collaborator, Ivan Ponting, would like to thank:

Pat, Rosie and Joe Ponting

Di Law for the bacon butties

Ian Marshall for his assured and sensitive editing

Rhea Halford and Rory Scarfe of Simon & Schuster

The designer Imran Haq

Andy Cowie of Colorsport, Mark Leech at Offside, David Scripps, Vito Inglese and Alex Waters of the Daily Mirror, Alan Pinnock and Louisa Nolan at the Daily Mail, John Peters of Manchester United and Getty Images, Hayley Newman at Getty Images, Lucie Gregory at the Press Association, Billy Robertson at Action Images

Mark Wylie at the Manchester United Museum
Les Gold
David Welch